"I believe what we need to do, ... the Holy Spirit'. Jeannie Morga... powerful."

 – Canon J.John

"Jeannie is a popular speaker at Soul Survivor youth and adult conferences around the world. She writes as she speaks, naturally, candidly, providing good teaching on the ministry of the Holy Spirit and illustrating it with many helpful experiences."

 – Bishop David Pytches

"Jeannie's new book Encounter the Holy Spirit is practical, powerful and a manual for anyone wanting to know the power and presence of the Holy Spirit and to understand more practically how to pray for others.

 "I am so thankful for this book. It moved me deeply and reminded me again how amazing the power of God is, and that He is mighty to save and that He comes to live in us by His Holy Spirit. Dive in and discover this truth for your life and for the lives of others around you today."

 – Beth Redman

"Over the years I've learnt so much from Jeannie regarding ministering in the power of the Holy Spirit. This helpful book will equip anyone wanting to step out and learn more."

 – Tim Hughes

"Jeannie Morgan is a humble, sensitive and faithful co-worker with the Holy Spirit. In this book she unpacks how an extraordinary God works with and through ordinary people to bring His gifts of life, healing and freedom. Rooted in a deep understanding of the Holy Spirit and in years of experience, this book will equip you to join in God's great adventure of being and bringing His blessing and grace to others."

 – David Westlake

Encounter the Holy Spirit

Jeannie Morgan

MONARCH
BOOKS

Oxford, UK, and Grand Rapids, Michigan, USA

First published in the UK in 2011 by Monarch Books (a publishing imprint of Lion Hudson plc) and by Elevation (a publishing imprint of the Memralife Group):
Lion Hudson plc, Wilkinson House, Jordan Hill Road, Oxford OX2 8DR
Tel: +44 (0)1865 302750; Fax +44 (0)1865 302757;
email monarch@lionhudson.com; www.lionhudson.com
Memralife Group, 14 Horsted Square, Uckfield, East Sussex TN22 1QG
Tel: +44 (0)1825 746530; Fax +44 (0)1825 748899;
www.elevationmusic.com

ISBN 978 0 85721 168 2 (print)
ISBN 978 0 85721 196 5 (epub)
ISBN 978 0 85721 195 8 (Kindle)
ISBN 978 0 85721 197 2 (PDF)

Distributed by:
UK: Marston Book Services, PO Box 269, Abingdon, Oxon, OX14 4YN
USA: Kregel Publications, PO Box 2607, Grand Rapids, Michigan 49501

British Library Cataloguing Data
A catalogue record for this book is available from the British Library

Printed and bound in the UK by Clays Ltd, St Ives plc.

I dedicate this book to my wonderful grandchildren
Harry, Charlie, Ted and Marybeth.
You inspire me and show me Jesus
through a child's eyes.

contents

ACKNOWLEDGMENTS

I want to take this opportunity to thank those who have modelled the nature and work of the Holy Spirit to me in so many ways: David Pytches, Mary Pytches, and Mike Pilavachi.

David, you have never stopped encouraging me since the first day I met you. Thank you for being so bold in those early days, for all the risks you took, not worrying about your own reputation as you released us, your congregation, into the ministry of the Holy Spirit. You were and are an amazing leader and I value your words of wisdom and friendship. Thank you for your helpful comments and encouraging me in getting this book published.

Mary, my friend, you are an inspiration to me. Thank you so much for those early days of ministering the healing of Jesus into my inner pain. You have studied, modelled and taught so much in the area of inner healing. Thank you for sharing and releasing what you have learnt to me and to so many others. You have both demonstrated such rich values of prayer ministry. For that, and your always "open door", I am truly thankful.

Mike, since Ken and I started working with you in the church youth group seventeen years ago, life has certainly never been dull! Thank you for the way you have always encouraged me. I love the way that you never settle, but are always seeking more of Jesus. You continue to surprise, inspire and challenge me in the way you interact with the Holy Spirit and the way you put your reputation on the line. Your passion and love for Jesus (and for people) is infectious. You are always seeking to lift Jesus up instead of yourself. It's a great model of leadership. Thank you for the many opportunities you have given me at Soul Survivor and for putting up with my nagging! I really value your friendship.

Ken, you are my faithful husband and best friend. Thank you

for the many ways you assist, support and enable me. Together we have enjoyed so many exciting adventures encountering the Holy Spirit. You look after me so well – you really are my other half, making up for my many weaknesses. I promise to stop talking about this book now!

In getting this book published I would like to thank the following people: Wendy Beech-Ward for a very timely conversation that caused you to start a whirlwind of action! The staff at Elevation and at Monarch Books: thank you for all you did in such a short space of time. Particular thanks to Tony Collins who worked with such efficiency and communicated so well. And of course thank you to Tim Pettingale, who edited it at top speed.

But for all these things the glory belongs to you, Jesus! Thank *you* for sending the Holy Spirit.

FOREWORD

This is a timely book. At a time when we appear to have won the old charismatic battle but lost the charismatic war, the Church desperately needs the teaching contained in these pages.

Most Christians believe in the gift of tongues, but very few know how and why they should exercise the gift regularly. Many of us believe the gift of prophecy is still for today, but churches and individuals who exercise a regular and effective prophetic ministry are few and far between. We believe that Jesus can heal people today, but the only real models many believers see are either a formal prayer of intercession or the white-suited celebrity doing all the "magic" from the stage. We desperately need not only to teach but also to equip the Church – to move in the manifest presence of, and minister in, the power of the Holy Spirit.

This book sets out to do just that. Jeannie is not first of all a theologian (although she knows her Bible), or a teacher (although she teaches regularly and effectively at our church and our conferences). She is, most of all, a practitioner. Jeannie has been doing all this stuff for years. That is why this book is above all practical. It is sensible, biblical, warm and down to earth. The gifts of the Spirit are not only explained; we are enabled to begin exercising them.

I have known and served alongside Jeannie Morgan and her husband Ken for nearly thirty years. Jeannie lives out consistently and effectively all that she has written about here, doing so in the context and under the authority of the local church. I and my fellow hosts at the Soul Survivor festivals have a little game. During ministry times we play not "Where's Wally" but "Where's Jeannie"! We follow the trail of wonderful devastation in the crowd to find the little spiritual atomic bomb laying hands on anyone in the way.

We need to be filled by the Spirit and move in the power of the Spirit if we are to effectively evangelise and disciple our nation. We also need the values and practices that we see in scripture. I am not sure what is worse, a dry, boring powerless evangelicalism that knows how to think but has no idea how to feel, or a hyped-up, manipulative, dishonest charismaticism that seems to think that asking questions and thinking are the enemies of the Spirit! We must embrace the radical middle that we find modelled by Jesus and the early Church. We need to be naturally supernatural, remembering that the greatest healing is the forgiveness of sins and the most wonderful miracle is the conversion that leads to salvation. We need to understand the biblical concept of whole body ministry, and the truth that when it comes to the ministry Jesus gave his Church, everyone gets to play – but we need to play nicely, and share the toys!

I pray that *Encounter the Holy Spirit* will prove a useful tool in helping you to move in the gifts and power that are Jesus' charismata (gifts of grace) to you.

Mike Pilavachi
Soul Survivor

WHAT IS THIS BOOK ABOUT?

I am passionate about the Holy Spirit! For many years I have spoken to teens and adults in churches and seminars, encouraging them to get to know Him better. When we are equipped to minister in the freedom He brings, we will know His power to preach the gospel, heal the sick, cast out demons and raise the dead!

There are already some excellent books on the person, work and gifts of the Holy Spirit, and these will offer you a good grounding in understanding the theology around the subject. Over the last few years, however, I have become increasingly aware that people are hungry to learn more about being *equipped* in the Holy Spirit's power, and that is why I have written this book. In it, I hope to answer questions such as:

- What gifts has He given me?
- How do I hear what the Holy Spirit is saying?
- How do I take steps to minister to others?

I have purposely made this book as practical and accessible as possible. The following pages are not an academic study, but are written to encourage you to jump into an adventure with God. The same power that raised Jesus Christ from the dead lives in you and you have full access to it!

The Holy Spirit wants to use *you*!

Are you ready to start your own adventure?

CHAPTER 1

GETTING TO KNOW THE HOLY SPIRIT

With the index finger of your right hand, draw an imaginary number six in the air. At the same time, with your right foot draw an imaginary circle in a clockwise direction.

If all goes according to plan, you should discover that almost immediately your foot starts to form a circle in an *anti*-clockwise direction. No matter how much you try, you can't easily make it go in a clockwise direction. Watching someone trying to do it is very amusing. It should be so simple, but if you are the one participating it is actually very difficult. It remains a mystery why your body cannot obey something that your brain is telling it to do.

What has all this to do with the Holy Spirit, you may ask?

Well, we are created holistically – body, mind, soul and spirit. As the above illustration shows, to say that we should understand or achieve everything with our brains is inadequate. Sometimes, we need to accept that things happen in and around us that we can't explain.

God is Spirit. He reveals Himself to us through the Holy Spirit in ways that are not always easily understood. He will sometimes speak or act "Spirit to spirit", or touch our emotions in ways we can't logically explain. He frequently chooses to do things in very different ways to the ways we would choose to do them. This is not so that He can ambush us or shock us, but because He knows what we need better than we know ourselves.

GOD IS THREE-IN-ONE

When we talk about God we are effectively speaking of three persons. He is God the Father, God the Son, who is Jesus Christ our Redeemer, and God the Holy Spirit, who is our Comforter and Guide.

This is the biggest mystery in the universe. Perhaps it will help, for now, to see the Godhead as similar to a married couple: distinct personalities joined together as one. Neither person loses their uniqueness in a marriage, but is linked closely through a love relationship. The Father, Son and Holy Spirit are all unique, separate and complete – but they are one.

It is a difficult concept to understand and because much of God remains a mystery, we are unlikely to ever fully grasp the workings of the Trinity. If we could, we would be just like God!

THE ATTRACTION OF THE SUPERNATURAL

As human beings we are fascinated by the world of the supernatural. Have you noticed how many movies, books and television programmes have their roots in it? Even tiny children are exposed to the concept that there is a power at work outside of themselves through a steady stream of visual entertainment. The programme *Wonder Pets*, aimed at two-year-olds, is all about little animated animals who possess supernatural powers and who act like superheroes.

From an early age we have all been encouraged to accept that supernatural power is something "make believe". What begins with the tooth fairy and Santa Claus progresses, as we get older, to darker images of witchcraft and wizardry. We are being fed images and stories that instruct us in the evil side of the supernatural. For some people, the fascination with the darker side is all consuming and they find it too easy to get drawn into an altogether more dangerous world. At the very least, it can make it more difficult for us to be open to the supernatural power of God.

Sometimes it can seem like the devil has claimed the rights to the supernatural world. In films, we are shown stories of characters who are either good or evil. Towards the end, it often seems as if good just about overcomes evil. This gives people the impression that the forces of good are not very powerful, as they only just manage to overcome the forces of evil – as if it could have gone either way right until the end. This may sell films at the box office, but it can seriously affect our thinking when we consider the power of God in relation to evil.

A MOMENT TO CLARIFY SOMETHING

I want to take some time to make sure we have things in perspective.

God is not the equal opposite to Satan!

God is the Almighty. He is supreme and He is sovereign. There is no one and nothing at all like Him on earth or under the earth or above the earth. The power of God is higher and greater than any other power – full stop! It may help you to think of the shape of a triangle. God is at the top and Satan is at the bottom as a fallen angel. His status is equal but opposite to that of a heavenly archangel.

God made all creation and this included the angels. We know from Genesis that everything God made was good. Many theologians believe that Satan was a beautiful angel who God appointed to be in charge of other angels. In these verses from Isaiah chapter 14 he is called the "morning star", translated from the word "Lucifer":

How you have fallen from heaven, morning star, son of the dawn! You have been cast down to the earth, you who once laid low the nations! You said in your heart, "I will ascend to the heavens; I will raise my throne above the stars of God; I will sit enthroned on the mount of assembly, on the utmost heights of Mount Zaphon. I will ascend above the tops of

*the clouds; I will make myself like the Most High." But you
are brought down to the realm of the dead, to the depths of
the pit.*

Isaiah 14:12–15

At some point during his rule over the other angels, Satan became proud and decided that he wanted the angels to worship *him* instead of God. Some of them did, resulting in them being cast out of heaven by God. These fallen angels are referred to as evil spirits or demons. Other passages you could look up to learn more about this are Ezekiel 28:12–17 and 2 Corinthians 11:14.

In the Bible we can see that the devil (the name most familiar for him in the New Testament) is allowed to pass in and out of God's presence until the day when he will be utterly banished. This day will be when Jesus finally returns to earth.

The Bible teaches us that the devil is limited in what he can do. In Job 1:6–12 and 2:1–7 it is clear that he has to effectively ask God for permission before doing anything specifically involving God's people:

*The Lord said to Satan, "Very well, then, everything he has
is in your power, but on the man himself do not lay a finger."
Then Satan went out from the presence of the Lord.*

Job 1:12

And in the New Testament:

Simon, Simon, Satan has asked to sift all of you as wheat.

Luke 22:31

So Be at Peace!

I want to encourage you: in a world where people's preoccupation with the supernatural binds them to live filled with fear, as

Christians we need have no fear of Satan or his evil spirits. Our God is higher!

Satan hates the name of Jesus, but had no choice but to submit to it by the work of the cross. When Jesus died on the cross, Satan was defeated, but he is yet to be destroyed. This will happen when Jesus finally returns.

This can be illustrated further with the following analogy: at the end of the Second World War, when the Allied forces landed at Normandy in France, everyone knew that this was a good sign that the war was won. It was to be called "D-Day". The enemy knew he was defeated. Key towns and cities were reclaimed and there was some celebration as a result.

However, battles were still being fought here and there, as the enemy had not been completely overthrown. It was not until "VE Day", when the Germans finally admitted defeat, that there was widespread jubilation. The enemy was finally destroyed – the war was over. So it will be when Jesus comes back to earth and Satan is destroyed. There will be a new heaven and a new earth. Every knee will bow and every tongue will proclaim that Jesus is Lord. In the meantime, there are still battles to be fought.

THE AMAZING POWER OF GOD

I am intrigued by disaster movies. Not the *War of The Worlds* type, but films about natural disasters – those that involve volcanoes erupting, tornados swirling, tidal waves crashing or earthquakes shaking. In the films, the actors rush around trying to divert or manage this huge release of natural power, but it is impossible! The force of the power and energy is too relentless – it is something beyond the control of man.

I love seeing God's power at work and in many ways it is just like the unstoppable forces described above. I can't understand how it all works – it is beyond my comprehension and control – but I can clearly see the effects of it in people's lives and the world I live in.

God's power can heal. God's power can change lives. God's power started the world. God's power can end it!

THE HOLY SPIRIT AND JESUS

I passionately want to tell you about the Holy Spirit, how you can get to know Him and also how you can be empowered by Him so that He can use you just as He used the disciples to do His work.

We read in the New Testament how Jesus had a ministry of preaching about the kingdom of God and we are told that signs and wonders followed. He promised too that

> *these signs will accompany those who believe: In my name they will drive out demons; they will speak in new tongues...*
> **Mark 16:17**

From the beginning of His ministry, Jesus taught His disciples to do as He did, being empowered by God through the Holy Spirit. Signs and wonders did not happen and will not happen through us without the presence of the Holy Spirit. We could try to perform them in our own strength, but would soon give up as we would be totally unsuccessful! But seeing miraculous signs by the power of the Holy Spirit should and can be a part of our everyday lives in Jesus.

Jesus taught His disciples how to heal the sick, cast out demons and raise the dead. In this way He demonstrated the good news of eternal life and showed how the world could be saved. God can empower us to do these same works of Jesus – in fact, He wants to. I know this is true because it has been my own experience and the experience of many people I know. The wonderful news today is that He wants to do this through you too. He wants to use you to be a catalyst for healing, deliverance, salvation and even raising people from the dead – all for His glory. I have not *yet* seen anyone raised from the dead, but I am definitely hoping I will see that too!

There is a story about the wife of the evangelist Smith Wigglesworth, who was apparently very annoyed after she was raised from the dead by her husband – she was very happy where she was and didn't want to come back to earth!

I want to see all that God has available for us, received by us and activated. I am longing to see people not only becoming Christians, but also being healed from their past hurts. I long to see them receive wholeness. I am longing to see the church, the body of Christ, through children's groups, youth groups and adult congregations, be so empowered that people turn to Jesus for healing – either in their own personal prayers or through prayer ministry from other believers – before seeking comfort from other sources to numb their pain.

WHO IS tHe HOLY SPIRIt?

The Holy Spirit is God. We have read previously that He is the person and presence of God, part of the Trinity with the Father and the Son. He has a personality and a character, as we will see in the following chapters of this book.

The Holy Spirit is first mentioned at the beginning of the Bible in the events of creation. In Genesis 1:2 we are told:

Now the earth was formless and empty, darkness was over the surface of the deep, and the Spirit of God was hovering over the waters.

Genesis 1:2

We are told that the world was without any form. It was dark and empty. But the Holy Spirit was hovering over the waters. Can you imagine what that must have looked like? I wonder if He made all the water churn up like a tremendous tsunami as He started to divide the mass of water into oceans, seas, rivers, lakes and waterfalls. It must have been an incredible sight.

The most powerful mass of water I have ever seen was at Niagara Falls. The noise was deafening. It was a breathtaking sight and so powerful that even the river, as it approached the falls, was bubbling and swirling at a tremendous speed. Yes, it was awesome, but nothing compared to what the Holy Spirit was doing at the beginning of creation.

In the Old Testament the Holy Spirit is often referred to as the Spirit of God and there are many instances of Him doing incredible things. However, for the purposes of this book we will be looking at the work of the Holy Spirit in the New Testament.

THE HOLY SPIRIT IN THE NEW TESTAMENT

In just a few pages of the New Testament we encounter the Holy Spirit in many dramatic ways.

Jesus was conceived by the Holy Spirit in the womb of the Virgin Mary. At His baptism, Jesus came up out of the water and the Holy Spirit descended upon Him as a dove. Then He was led by the Holy Spirit into the desert and was tempted by Satan.

Jesus did not need baptism for the forgiveness of sins, since He was perfect and without sin. He asked to be baptized by John in order to identify fully with mankind. Jesus chose to become fully man when He came to earth from heaven. He chose to lay aside His divine attributes, such as being able to be everywhere at the same time and knowing everything about everyone. He opted for being empowered through the anointing of the Holy Spirit.

The Holy Spirit's descent upon Him was also a visual aid to everyone present to show that this was no ordinary man, but the Son of God. The whole drama of the occasion was completed when His Father spoke from heaven and affirmed Him as His beloved Son and everyone present could hear how pleased He was with Him.

> *When all the people were being baptized, Jesus was*
> *baptized too. And as he was praying, heaven was opened*
> *and the Holy Spirit descended on him in bodily form like*
> *a dove. And a voice came from heaven: "You are my Son,*
> *whom I love; with you I am well pleased."*

Luke 3:21–22

So it was the Holy Spirit who empowered Jesus to heal the sick and do many signs and wonders. The Holy Spirit later also raised Jesus from the dead. This same Holy Spirit also came upon the disciples at Pentecost and empowered them to do the works of Jesus. The *same* Holy Spirit wants to empower *us* to do these *same* things.

You may ask, what for? Why does He want us to do the things Jesus did? Because there is a needy world that still needs to be touched by God's power and made aware of His presence, and also because signs and wonders glorify Jesus when people see them happening. Signs and wonders make Jesus become bigger in our eyes. The Bible refers to this as *magnifying* Him. When we know we serve a big, powerful God, it gives us a boldness to speak to unbelievers about the kingdom of God. Being empowered by the Holy Spirit also enables us to remain obedient to the commands of Jesus.

MY STORY

I love the Holy Spirit! I would never have known Jesus without Him and neither would you. This is the story of how I first met the Holy Spirit and realized that someone outside of me was at work.

I didn't know Jesus, but if you had described to me the nature and character of the Holy Spirit I would have recognized who it was that was working. Unfortunately, at that time no one knew what was going on with me, so no one was able to explain!

Some years ago we had a tragedy happen in our family. As

I was answering the front door to our eldest child, unbeknown to me our youngest daughter Joanna had fallen into our small swimming pool at the back of our house and was drowned. As you can imagine, we were completely devastated. At that time neither I nor my husband were Christians. In fact, I was very anti-God because our first child was stillborn and I had blamed God for this (the full story is recounted in my previous book *Let the Healing Begin,* Kingsway, 2007).

After Joanna died, one of the earliest visitors to our house was the local vicar, David Pytches. If I am honest, I really didn't feel very welcoming towards him, but he had come to offer his condolences and leave a Bible with us. I decided to take him into our kitchen rather than making him more comfortable in the lounge. After some conversation and while we were still standing in our kitchen, he asked if he could pray before he left. We agreed to it and as he prayed he asked Jesus to come into the kitchen by the power of the Holy Spirit. "How odd!" I thought. "Surely Jesus is in church and He doesn't come into kitchens!" As David left I thanked him for coming and explained that I thought that as vicars go, he was a nice enough man, but I didn't want anything he had to offer!

WHEN THINGS BEGAN TO CHANGE

After David left us I noticed that every time I went into the kitchen I experienced a warmth that was nothing to do with either the oven or the central heating. It soon became a place in which I wanted to spend time, which was quite unusual for me. I found myself drawn by something that I had no explanation for. I felt safe there.

Added to this, I was also experiencing something strange in the house. It was as if there were two hands suspended in space that were drawing me forward, and if I closed my eyes I could clearly see them. If I had my eyes open I just had this huge impression of something or someone drawing me somewhere that was safe. I realized that if I mentioned this to anyone they would probably sedate me, thinking that the shock had finally made me flip! If only I could have spoken to a Christian, they would probably have explained that one of the jobs of the Holy Spirit is to lead us safely into truth – to lead us to Jesus.

My husband and I also were aware that something was happening to us for which we had no language. We seemed to be able to offer peace and comfort to others without really trying. Friends and relatives visited us in great distress and seemed to go away feeling comforted. We were obviously grieving ourselves, but it felt as though in our pain we were being comforted on a whole new level. We couldn't work out how that could be happening. Again, we had no idea that the Holy Spirit is also spoken of in the Bible as the Comforter.

My husband said one day, "I think it's all those Christians down the road at the church. I think they are praying for us and some sort of electricity is being released upon us that is affecting us." I agreed, as there seemed to be no other explanation. Little did we know that a far greater power was at work than electricity!

As I started to arrange the details regarding Joanna's funeral, I began to see pictures in my head. Once I saw a lovely white dress like a wedding dress and knew without a doubt that all those invited to the funeral should come as if they were coming to a wedding: *Joanna's wedding*. I had no idea at that point that in the Bible Jesus is spoken of as the Bridegroom and the church as His bride.

JOANNA'S WEDDING

I needed a dress to wear for Joanna's funeral. There was only one clothes shop near our village that sold ladies' clothes. The main town was ten miles away and I didn't want to make the journey there, so one day as I walked past this little old-fashioned shop I felt the impulse to go in.

I am very short and find it difficult to get clothes that look right on me, so imagine my surprise when I walked over to a rail of dresses and skirts and saw the perfect dress. It was as if a light-cream coloured dress was shouting to me, "This is it!" I picked it up and didn't even try it on. I knew this was my dress for our daughter's funeral.

As I walked outside the shop, dress in hand, another picture came into my head. This time it was a circle of white flowers of a type I had never seen before. They were long and beautiful and the words in my head were that the circle was symbolic of eternity and that the long stems of the flowers were reaching out to others. At that point I had a "knowing" deep inside me that the death of Joanna was going to reach out and enable others to know eternity. I had no idea at this time what this meant, as I had no knowledge of Jesus or the Bible.

I walked into the florist's shop next door to the dress shop and my eyes immediately rested on a bucket containing white flowers exactly like the ones in my picture. I drew the picture I had seen in my head and gave it to the florist, ordering it for display on the top of Joanna's coffin.

The next morning as I woke up, many words were forming in my head. Immediately I wrote down my thoughts about the life of Joanna that I wanted to be read out at her funeral.

Although we were not Christians then, her funeral was beautiful. It was unlike any funeral I or my family and friends had ever been to. The chapel was full of light and packed with people. The Holy Spirit was present, comforting us and others through us. It will stay in my memory as Joanna's wedding day because it was the day we "gave her" to Jesus. Of course, we did then go through a long grieving process, but every step of the way the Holy Spirit did not leave me, leading me lovingly into the arms of Jesus so that I started to get to know Him as my Healer, and later on as my Saviour and my Lord. I started to read the Bible, learning truths from Scripture, and began to go to the local church.

I have to tell you that the picture I was given of the flowers was fulfilled. Seven people in my family so far have become Christians. Hundreds of others have been affected when they have heard my testimony, opening themselves to the Holy Spirit and receiving healing.

HOW the HOLY SPIRIt LeaDS US

The Bible says that the Holy Spirit leads us into truth, and after Joanna's death this was what was happening to me. He was leading me into the truth *about* Jesus, as well as leading me to the truth that *is* Jesus. Jesus is the truth, saying of Himself, "I am the way and the truth and the life" (John 14:6).

I love the passage about the Holy Spirit in Ephesians that says:

> *And you also were included in Christ when you heard the message of truth, the gospel of your salvation. When you believed, you were marked in him with a seal, the promised Holy Spirit...*

Ephesians 1:13

Further on it says:

> *I keep asking that the God of our Lord Jesus Christ, the glorious Father, may give you the Spirit of wisdom and revelation, so that you may know him better.*

Ephesians 1:17

We can see that the Holy Spirit gives us wisdom and revelation so that we can know the Father better. Jesus and the Father are one, so we can know them more fully by revelation from the Holy Spirit. This passage is also speaking about being empowered by the Holy Spirit. It continues:

I pray that the eyes of your heart may be enlightened in order that you may know the hope to which he has called you, the riches of his glorious inheritance in his holy people...

Ephesians 1:18

This was what was happening to me after our child drowned. The Holy Spirit was enlightening my heart, giving me hope.

The passage continues to its finale:

... and his incomparably great power for us who believe. That power is the same as the mighty strength he exerted when he raised Christ from the dead and seated him at his right hand in the heavenly realms, far above all rule and authority, power and dominion...

Ephesians 1:19–21

The incomparably great power from Father God, via the Holy Spirit, that raised Jesus from the dead and seated Him at the right hand of the Father, is the same incomparably great power that is available to those who believe! That means you and me, if you believe and confess that Jesus died and rose again for the forgiveness of your sins.

We also see from these verses that we have been *marked* with the Holy Spirit, labelled as with a seal, similar to the hallmark we see on gold or silver. He is a "deposit" guaranteeing what is to come, bringing wisdom and revelation and also this incomparable power.

MORE ROLES OF THE HOLY SPIRIT

If you search around in the New Testament you will also discover other attributes and activities of the Holy Spirit. I've listed some of them here:

- He comforts (John 14:26, NIV 1984).
- He counsels (John 14:26; 16:7, KJV).
- He is the Spirit of Truth (John 16:13–14).
- He teaches (John 14:26).
- He guides into truth (John 16:13).
- He speaks (John 16:13; Acts 1:2).
- He anoints (Luke 4:18; Acts 10:38).
- He empowers (Acts 2).
- He gives gifts (1 Corinthians 12:1–11).
- He bears fruit (Galatians 5:22).
- He convicts people of sin (John 16:8).
- He delivers (Romans 8:2).
- He sends (Mark 1:12).
- He gives birth (John 3:6, 8).
- He gives life (John 6:63).
- He prophesies (Acts 11:28).
- He intercedes (Romans 8:26).
- He works signs and miracles (Romans 15:19).
- He makes people holy and whole (Romans 15:16).
- He declares (John 16:13–14).
- He hears (John 16:13–14).

He is not confined to this list, of course. He does much, much more, but you do not need to take my word for it. Look for yourself in the Bible and you will discover more truth. We must expect the Holy Spirit to do all of the above and more *for us* and *through us* for others. And for God's glory!

The wonderful thing is that as we get to know the Holy Spirit we can recognize when He is prompting us or speaking to us about something. Everyone will hear differently. For me this sounds the same as my voice, but it is compelling. It feels as if there is a "take notice" dimension to it.

This year and every year at Soul Survivor Festivals, I have seen the Holy Spirit do the things He did in the New Testament, apart from raising the dead. The Holy Spirit has ministered during times of prayer ministry through different kinds of miracles, salvations, healings, deliverances from evil spirits, prophecy, words of knowledge, discernment of spirits, anointing and the gift of tongues.

And guess what? God used people just like you and me to do all that stuff. He wants everyone who loves Him to partner with Him in all of it!

PRAYER

Jesus, I really want to know the Holy Spirit. Not just what He does, but who He is. I want to invite You, Holy Spirit, to teach me more of Yourself and lead me closer to Jesus. I choose to believe now that You want to use me like You used the first disciples. In the stillness of this place now, please open up my understanding as I surrender myself to You. I receive all that You want to give me, with a thankful heart. Amen.

ACTION

As you read this book, the Holy Spirit wants to speak to you and change your expectations of what He can and will do through you.

What would you like to say to Him now?

Is there anything that you are anxious about?

SCRIPTURES

Jesus returned to Galilee in the power of the Spirit, and news about him spread through the whole countryside. He was teaching in their synagogues, and everyone praised him.

He went to Nazareth, where he had been brought up, and on the Sabbath day he went into the synagogue, as was his custom. He stood up to read, and the scroll of the prophet Isaiah was handed to him. Unrolling it, he found the place where it is written: "The Spirit of the Lord is on me..."

Luke 4:14–18

Again Jesus said, "Peace be with you! As the Father has sent me, I am sending you." And with that he breathed on them and said, "Receive the Holy Spirit."

John 20:21–22

Do you not know that your bodies are temples of the Holy Spirit, who is in you, whom you have received from God?

1 Corinthians 6:19

I am going to send you what my Father has promised; but stay in the city until you have been clothed with power from on high.

Luke 24:49

"Let anyone who is thirsty come to me and drink. Whoever believes in me, as Scripture has said, rivers of living water will flow from within them." By this he meant the Spirit, whom those who believed in him were later to receive. Up to that time the Spirit had not been given, since Jesus had not yet been glorified.

John 7:37–39

Very truly I tell you, no one can enter the kingdom of God unless they are born of water and the Spirit.

John 3:5

CHAPTER 2

BEING FILLED TO OVERFLOWING

Jesus knew who He was and what He had come to earth to do. At His baptism He was not only immersed in water by John, but was filled with the Holy Spirit by His Father in heaven. Jesus' ministry was dependent on Him being filled with the Holy Spirit and He could do nothing without Him.

Jesus returned to Galilee in the power of the Spirit, and news about him spread through the whole countryside. He was teaching in their synagogues, and everyone praised him.

Luke 4:14–15

Jesus then made it clear to His disciples that the same was true for them:

On one occasion, while he was eating with them, he gave them this command: "Do not leave Jerusalem, but wait for the gift my Father promised, which you have heard me speak about. For John baptized with water, but in a few days you will be baptized with the Holy Spirit."

Acts 1:4–5

set apart

Jesus knew that the power of God was upon Him. He knew that He was anointed and set apart for a purpose. One of the definitions of "anointed" is *chosen*.

Do you know that you are also chosen? You are set apart for a purpose. God has made His Holy Spirit available to you to anoint and equip you to do something specific, something special, that only *you* can do. There is no way that any of us could do anything significant for God without the same presence and power in our lives that Jesus had.

For God, who said, "Let light shine out of darkness," made his light shine in our hearts to give us the light of the knowledge of God's glory displayed in the face of Christ. But we have this treasure in jars of clay to show that this all-surpassing power is from God and not from us.

2 Corinthians 4:6–7

Of course, this means that whenever we minister to people in signs and wonders, we don't take any of the glory for ourselves, because it is not *our* power that does it but *God's* through us.

We are supposed to live lives that imitate the life of Jesus. As He was anointed and appointed to heal the sick, raise the dead, and cast out demons through the power of the Holy Spirit, so are we. God has generously chosen us to continue the ministry of Jesus. He said in John chapter 14 that He would not leave us alone when He went back to heaven, but instead the Holy Spirit would come for everyone:

I will not leave you as orphans; I will come to you.

John 14:18

DIFFERENT KINDS OF FILLINGS

When we first become a Christian we receive the Holy Spirit as part of the salvation gift package. We read about this happening to the disciples when Jesus appeared to them after being raised from the dead. Jesus says to them:

> *Again Jesus said, "Peace be with you! As the Father has sent me, I am sending you." And with that he breathed on them and said, "Receive the Holy Spirit..."*
>
> **John 20:21–22**

This happened before Pentecost in Acts, when they had an altogether different experience of the filling of the Holy Spirit, which we shall explore in the next chapter.

As the disciples followed Jesus, He commanded them to heal the sick and cast out demons. He gave them power and authority to do this in His name. They watched Him, learned from Him and exercised the gifts of the Holy Spirit because they were part of His "team". At that point, their ministry was attached to the person of Jesus and mainly limited to the locality He was in.

It is a bit like working for a company like Marks and Spencer. To be part of the team, you are required to wear a uniform to distinguish your company loyalty and make you easily recognizable to shoppers.

The disciples were distinguishable as followers of Jesus because they were learning to do the things He did that made Him unique. Jesus was their encouragement, their teacher, their leader and their role model. But He knew He would not always be around in the flesh, so something else had to happen. A new filling was needed to empower them to continue His ministry long after He returned to be with His Father.

Jesus knew what it was because it had been revealed to Him by the Father. After the resurrection He said to His disciples:

I am going to send you what my Father has promised; but stay in the city until you have been clothed with power from on high.

Luke 24:49

Something different was coming, a new kind of filling, and the disciples were asked to wait for it. Notice that they were told to stay in the city until *He* arrives. The Holy Spirit is a power from on high but He is also a person. It is important that we remember to not just treat Him as a catalyst for signs and wonders; rather, we should honour Him at all times as a person.

SO WHO Gets the HOLY SPIRIT?

You may be reading this and thinking, "I couldn't do that stuff, casting out demons and healing the sick. I am not a good enough Christian. God wouldn't use me to do any of that." Well, that sort of thinking is untrue and unbiblical. Look at what Jesus says:

Which of you fathers, if your son asks for a fish, will give him a snake instead? Or if he asks for an egg, will give him a scorpion? If you then, though you are evil, know how to give good gifts to your children, how much more will your Father in heaven give the Holy Spirit to those who ask him!

Luke 11:11–13

Who are the people who will be given the Holy Spirit? The answer from the Bible is: *those who ask!*

It is as simple as that. There is not a select group of special people who are the only ones who can receive the Holy Spirit. God said:

I will pour out my Spirit on all people.

Acts 2:17

It is as clear as it can be: God wants us *all* to know the power and presence of His Holy Spirit, whoever we are and whatever we have done.

THE HOLY SPIRIT IS GOOD FOR YOU!

In Chapter 1 we considered how the increase in fascination with the supernatural can affect our thinking about the authority and goodness of God. We may think that if we ask for something supernatural from God, He will give us something we don't like, or something that has a sinister edge.

But the verses we've already read in Luke 11 tell us otherwise: "... how much more will your Father in heaven give the Holy Spirit to those who ask him!" We need to take Him at His word. God is not going to give you something that is the opposite of what you are asking Him for! If you ask Him for the Holy Spirit, He is not going to give you something evil. He is not going to give you something that will hurt or frighten you. He is a good God who loves to give His children good things. If you feel that you are not a good enough Christian to receive what God wants to give you, then just take a moment now to say this prayer:

> Please come, Holy Spirit, and fill me. Jesus, for
> some reason I don't think You will use me or give me
> Your power. I bring these feelings that I am not good
> enough to You. I bring to You now those beliefs that
> are not from You and leave them with You at the cross.
> I confess these sins to You and turn away from them.
> I receive from You the truth that You will pour Your
> Spirit out on all people. Fill me now with the truth of
> who You are and what You can do. Amen.

God has heard you and will answer.

GOD KNOWS YOU

Everyone is different. Some people are extrovert and loud, some are introvert and quiet. God knows you and knows how best to fill you with His Spirit.

We may feel anxious or fearful when we see someone receiving the Holy Spirit in a noisy way, thinking that the same will happen to us. That is a terrible thought for an introvert! But if the person receiving is an extrovert, used to being naturally noisy, then this fits their personality and feels safe and normal. Likewise, when a more introverted person receives the Holy Spirit in a quieter way, the noisier person may doubt that anything is happening at all. This is not the case; it just reflects their individual response to what the Holy Spirit is doing.

I am a noisy person. If a couple of days pass by and I haven't had the opportunity to be noisy, I have to walk around the house singing or calling out to make sure everyone knows I am there. It is part of my personality; I am an extrovert. When the Holy Spirit fills me, I can react in a loud way. I am not trying to draw attention to myself; it is just the way I am. I understand that for some people, my reactions to the Holy Spirit's filling can be disturbing at times!

We need to give room for each other to connect with the Holy Spirit in the way that feels the most freeing. We must not try to make someone's encounter with the Holy Spirit into something *we* want, as it is between that person and Him.

Just as I am rather noisy, my husband is generally more reserved. A true Englishman! When the Holy Spirit descends on him, his reaction is always very peaceful. The power of God is the same, but we have different responses and reactions to it.

BE FILLED TO OVERFLOWING

Before He ascended to heaven, Jesus said:

For John baptized with water, but in a few days you will be baptized with the Holy Spirit.

Acts 1:5

Baptism in the Holy Spirit should be the experience of every Christian. As we saw earlier in the chapter, the disciples operated with the power of the Holy Spirit *with* them as they accompanied Jesus in His ministry. It was only at Pentecost that they were truly empowered.

When we first become Christians the Holy Spirit dwells *in* us and we become a temple, or a house in which He can live. He begins to change us from the inside out. However, if we are to serve Him fully, we need our own time of Pentecost. We need the Holy Spirit to come *upon* us. If this doesn't happen, it is like a kettle plugged into a source of power but not switched on, so the power cannot flow to heat the water. Similarly, if a glove has no hand to fill it, it is useless and does not fulfil the purpose for which it was made.

When we are baptized in the Holy Spirit we are filled to overflowing with the power of God. In Greek, the word "baptize" means "to drench, soak, sink or overwhelm". It means being filled with the power of God and being filled with the presence of God.

HOW THE APOSTLE PAUL HANDLED IT

When amazing things were happing in Samaria in Acts chapter 8, Paul and John were sent by the church in Jerusalem to check it out. People were receiving Jesus, being delivered of demons, being healed and baptized.

> *When the apostles in Jerusalem heard that Samaria*
> *had accepted the word of God, they sent Peter and John*
> *to Samaria. When they arrived, they prayed for the new*
> *believers there that they might receive the Holy Spirit,*
> *because the Holy Spirit had not yet come on any of them;*
> *they had simply been baptized in the name of the Lord*
> *Jesus. Then Peter and John placed their hands on them,*
> *and they received the Holy Spirit.*

Acts 8:14–17

Paul knew that in addition to the Holy Spirit being received at the point of salvation, the new Christians needed a new filling to empower them to minister in the same way Jesus did after His own baptism.

WHat IS It LIKe to Be FILLeD UP?

I can safely say that there is nothing like being filled with the Holy Spirit! Once you have experienced it you will never want anything else in your life. In Ephesians Paul writes:

> *Do not get drunk on wine, which leads to debauchery.*
> *Instead, be filled with the Spirit...*
>
> **Ephesians 5:18**

Believe me, if you experience a drunk-like state from being filled with the Holy Spirit, you will never want to be drunk with anything else in your life! There is no comparison.

When Paul writes "be filled", it literally means, "go on being filled with the Holy Spirit". It is not a one-off experience but a daily blessing. In John chapter 7 Jesus speaks about receiving the empowering of the Holy Spirit as being like a "drinking in". Streams of living water will "flow from within" and the way to receive Him is simply to "drink".

The Holy Spirit is meant to flow through us and this flow is activated by our obedience to God's call on our lives. If we are filled up and do not use what we are given, we become like a stagnant pond with stinking water. We are meant to be more like a lake, fed by a stream that is continually filled and flowing out. I would much rather be "flowing" than "stinky", wouldn't you?

MY LIFE-CHANGING HOLY SPIRIT EXPERIENCE

One Sunday we had invited two people, Debbie and Alex, for lunch at our home. They were part of a team visiting our church from California, led by the late John Wimber, founder of the Vineyard movement. Over lunch they began to tell us some stories of the tremendous things that had happened when they and their team had prayed for our youth group the previous evening. We thought that some of the stories sounded a bit wild, but out of curiosity we decided to go with them to the evening service. I remember that the preacher spoke about the widow from 2 Kings chapter 4 who kept filling her earthenware pots with oil until there were no pots left.

All the time the preacher was speaking I had an ache in my stomach that was getting worse. It felt like I had a huge lump there. In addition I was feeling very restless and agitated, thinking, "Hurry up and finish!" because I knew that something significant was about to happen to me. At last, the preacher finished by saying, "If anyone wants to come forward to serve the Lord, then come right now so that we can pray for you." As he spoke those words it was as if someone had put a firework under my backside! I leapt up from my seat, treading on everyone's feet in my haste to get to the front. I wanted to "serve the Lord", but didn't quite know what this meant. I kept thinking, "I don't want to be a missionary! Please don't send me to Africa or India!" (This was my interpretation of "serving the Lord".)

I joined a group of people who were kneeling by the altar rail. By now the ache from the lump in my stomach had reached enormous proportions. I was desperate for something to happen, but did not know what and had no idea of what was about to take place.

The preacher, Lonnie Frisbee (what a great name!) laid his hands on my head and invited the power of the Holy Spirit to fill me. Immediately I saw the most terrible blackness I had ever seen. It was so dark that the ache in my stomach rose up, and as I began to sink into this horrible blackness, I let out a long, blood-curdling scream. Reflecting on this later, I understood that this was the expression of my deep pain and grief over the death of our little girl Joanna.

Suddenly as the scream ended, everything changed. The darkness had completely disappeared and I could feel something bubbling up deep inside me like a stream – something beautiful and clean. As the bubbling continued it filled my throat and mouth until at the top of my voice I began to worship Jesus in a language unknown to me that sounded so beautiful. It felt like each sound was a sound of love for Him. I felt as if I could burst with the love that was filling my mind, my body, my spirit and my emotions. I felt so alive and so completely in love with Jesus.

After a long while of doing this I then did something that did not embarrass me at all at the time, although later I could not believe I had done such a thing. In front of the whole congregation I lifted my hands and arms up high in the air and shouted at the top of my voice, *'Jesus, I love You!'* I must explain at this point that I am talking about 1981 and at that time, the things I am telling you about were not generally common practice in the churches in England!

Looking around, it seemed that God was not only working in me but in the rest of the congregation. Some people were rolling on the floor laughing; others were falling about all over the place like they were drunk. A lady, normally confined to a wheelchair due to severe Multiple Sclerosis, was pushing her husband around in her wheelchair, grinning from ear to ear! Some were shaking uncontrollably, others were receiving the gift of tongues and many other healings were taking place. It was bizarre to watch but also amazing!

Debbie, who had been at our home for lunch, asked if she could pray for me. As soon as she began to speak, I felt the power of the Holy Spirit again. I began to stamp my right foot and I was aware of her breaking the power of something in me. I immediately felt free from something, leaving me calm and at peace. She continued to pray for me, asking the Holy Spirit to impart to me the gift of knowledge, which we will learn about in a later chapter of this book.

KEN'S LIFE-CHANGING HOLY SPIRIT EXPERIENCE

All the time this was happening to me, my husband Ken was resolutely sitting in his seat. Once Debbie had finished praying for me I decided to go back, find him and ask him if he would like prayer to receive the Holy Spirit. His response was a blunt, "No thanks. It's late and I want to go home and have my tea!" Ken had watched the mayhem all around him and wasn't too keen.

However, eventually Debbie and her husband were given permission to pray for him quietly in the aisle, so he did not feel exposed. As I watched, I could hardly believe what was happening. Instead of standing upright, Ken was standing at an impossible angle, leaning back with his body rigid from head to toe. It was as if an invisible person was holding him halfway between the floor and an upright position.

I was feeling excited, wondering what was happening to him. When he stood up I asked him, "Well, what happened?"

Looking his usual self, he replied, "Nothing. I'm going home for my tea now."

I couldn't believe it! What he had been doing was impossible (naturally speaking), but he didn't seem to realize it.

HEALING TOO!

Ken went off home and I continued walking around the church for a while watching the amazing things God was doing. Suddenly I started to get a severe backache. I had never suffered a back problem before, so I was curious as to why I had suddenly started to ache.

As soon as I got home I went to find Ken to talk about all the things that had happened during the evening. My backache suddenly became much more severe. I said to Ken, "How about laying your hands on me like those Californians were doing and asking Jesus to heal me?" At first he was a bit reluctant, but as he could see I was suffering, he agreed. As soon as he laid his hands on my back I felt this tremendous heat. Excitedly I told Ken, "Something is happening! I can feel heat coming from your hands which is affecting my back. The pain is going!" At first he didn't believe me, but then when I told him the pain was completely gone he looked a bit gob-smacked. Then I realized what must have happened and told him I believed he had received a gift of healing when Debbie and Alex prayed for him. I encouraged him to keep praying for people.

AND STILL MORE!

Receiving the gift of tongues was a very special thing for me. For the next two weeks I could hardly speak in English. I had to concentrate hard, as I was speaking for long periods of time in my wonderful new prayer language, expressing love for Jesus in a totally new way. In Chapter 6 we will look at this gift in more detail.

Also, I seemed to have a new gift of knowledge in the supernatural, as Debbie had prayed. One day, as I walked past the house of a Christian lady named Jane, whom I hardly knew, I had a strong sense that I should knock on her door. As she answered, I explained that I did not know why I was there, but I felt I should knock. Jane invited me in, saying that her father had died the previous night and her mother was there with her, full of grief. I knelt down by Jane's mother, and asked if I could pray for her. I copied what the Californians had done and invited the Holy Spirit to come and be present, and then asked Jesus to do what He wanted to do.

I prayed in my new prayer language and waited. After a while Jane's mother's face changed and looked very peaceful and beautiful. She looked up and said, "I just saw my husband in heaven with Jesus. It was wonderful. I am not worried about him now, because I know where he is."

This is just one example of how the Holy Spirit began to take me on a new journey to discover His power and presence as an overflow of His love in my life. As He kept filling me, I continued to give it away. You can learn to do the same!

PRAYER

Holy Spirit, it is amazing that You want to empower me just like You empowered the disciples. I want You to use me just like You used them. I want to bring glory to Jesus. Thank You, Jesus, for dying for me and sending the Holy Spirit so that I can do amazing things in Your name for Your glory. I don't want anything to be in the way of what You want to do in me or through me. Take from me any lack of self-worth or self-esteem. I surrender it You now. Amen.

ACTION

The baptism of the Holy Spirit is given to change us from the inside out and give us free access to the same power that Jesus had. In fact, in John's gospel (14:12), Jesus says we will do *more* than He did.

As you read my story of how the Holy Spirit changed me and my husband, what did you think?

Do you want the Holy Spirit to do the same for you?

Would you like to know more power flowing through your life?

SCRIPTURES

In the last days, God says, I will pour out my Spirit on all people. Your sons and daughters will prophesy, your young men will see visions, your old men will dream dreams.

Acts 2:17

On the last and greatest day of the festival, Jesus stood and said in a loud voice, "Let anyone who is thirsty come to me and drink. Whoever believes in me, as Scripture has said, rivers of living water will flow from within them." By this he meant the Spirit, whom those who believed in him were later to receive. Up to that time the Spirit had not been given, since Jesus had not yet been glorified.

John 7:37–39

Which of you fathers, if your son asks for a fish, will give him a snake instead? Or if he asks for an egg, will give him a scorpion? If you then, though you are evil, know how to give good gifts to your children, how much more will your Father in heaven give the Holy Spirit to those who ask him!

Luke 11:11–13

Jesus answered, "Very truly I tell you, no one can enter the kingdom of God unless they are born of water and the Spirit. Flesh gives birth to flesh, but the Spirit gives birth to spirit. You should not be surprised at my saying, 'You must be born again.' The wind blows wherever it pleases. You hear its sound, but you cannot tell where it comes from or where it is going. So it is with everyone born of the Spirit."

John 3:5–8

CHapter 3

RECEIVING THE HOLY SPIRIT

In Chapter 2 we looked at what it is to operate in the overflow of the Holy Spirit. In this chapter I want to take us on from there and consider our part in inviting Him to fill us. At the end of the chapter you will see there is a practical exercise which you can do alone, with a friend or in a group.

IT WILL BE GIVEN TO YOU

The Holy Spirit wants to be personally invited to fill us to overflowing. He will never force Himself on anyone, even though He knows that His presence will make our lives so much better. Jesus says:

> *Ask and it will be given to you; seek and you will find; knock and the door will be opened to you.*
>
> **Matthew 7:7**

All we need to do is ask God and He will do the giving. Sometimes it doesn't seem to happen at the time of asking, but God hears every prayer we pray and will answer. In fact, there are times when the Holy Spirit will fill a person unexpectedly, outside of the walls of a church. I know someone who was baptized by the Holy Spirit when he was digging over his compost heap at the bottom of his garden! A friend of mine called Ruth was in a supermarket buying a tin of peaches when the Holy Spirit filled her and she heard a heavenly host of angels singing!

It's not about me

It is important that we do not get obsessed with *getting* more and more power. Some people can get so caught up in the power encounter or in the manifestations of the Holy Spirit that they lose sight of what it is really all about.

Remember that the Holy Spirit is a person. We must not separate the *power* of the Holy Spirit from the *person* of the Holy Spirit. As we surrender more and more of ourselves to Jesus, He responds to our surrender. Glorifying Jesus is paramount, never losing sight of who He is and what He has done for us on the cross.

Getting to know the Holy Spirit means we will increase in our revelation of Jesus more and more. There is no competition in the Trinity! It is Jesus who the Holy Spirit reveals to us and with whom we must become fixated – our eyes on Him, rather than getting more power for ourselves. We need to be more and more available to be used as a vessel, offering ourselves to the Holy Spirit to be used by Him to glorify Jesus and to further the kingdom of God.

Let's look at Pentecost

I could not write a book on encountering the Holy Spirit and leave out the account of what happened to the disciples at Pentecost.

The word "Pentecost" comes from the Greek word for the number fifty and it was a Jewish festival which was celebrated fifty days after Passover.

In Acts chapter 1 the disciples were gathered together in one room, having been told by Jesus to wait in Jerusalem for what the Father had promised them. As we have seen, they had already experienced the Holy Spirit's saving, teaching, miracle-working power, but had not had the gift of being fully immersed or baptized in the Holy Spirit.

As they waited expectantly, they continued to pray together, not knowing what was about to happen. We are told that:

Suddenly a sound like the blowing of a violent wind came from heaven and filled the whole house where they were sitting. They saw what seemed to be tongues of fire that separated and came to rest on each of them. All of them were filled with the Holy Spirit and began to speak in other tongues as the Spirit enabled them.

Acts 2:2–4

The Holy Spirit had arrived! Everything was about to change and the gospel was going to be preached not just in Jerusalem but across the whole world.

For these disciples who had just seen Jesus ascend into heaven, this visitation of His presence by the Holy Spirit must have been amazing – just what they had been waiting for. This "waiting" is a crucial aspect of receiving the Holy Spirit either individually or corporately in a meeting of believers.

SYMBOLS OF the HOLY SPIRIt

There are many symbolic pictures of the Holy Spirit in the New Testament which help us understand how we can receive Him and how He operates in different contexts.

One of the first images in the New Testament is that of a *dove* which descends upon Jesus as He is baptized. Jesus Himself speaks of the Holy Spirit as a *gift*, then as *water* and *streams of living water*. As we have just seen, in Acts the Holy Spirit makes the sound of a violent *wind* and releases tongues of *fire*. Further on in Acts we read that the building the disciples were in was *shaken* by the Holy Spirit (Acts 4:31).

Let's look at some of these key symbols in more detail.

THE DOVE

There are a few things we need to consider concerning the baptism of Jesus. As He was being baptized by John, the Bible tells us that people saw heaven ripped apart and what appeared to be a dove descended on Him. As this happened, God the Father spoke from heaven, affirming that Jesus was His Son and that He was very pleased with Him.

When I first started to look at these symbolic pictures I asked myself, "Why a dove? Why not an eagle?" An eagle sounds more robust, exotic and powerful – a fitting symbol to represent the Holy Spirit.

I decided to look up the description of the dove in a book of birds I have at home. I read that a dove is a clean bird that likes to make its nest in a clean place.

Wow! There could be no cleaner place for a dove to rest than on Jesus! He is perfectly clean and perfectly pure.

Reading this made me want to be a clean place for the Holy Spirit to descend upon. Jesus makes us clean because of what He did on the cross – the blood of Jesus, God's Son, shed for me to cleanse me from all my sin (1 John 1:7).

I love the idea of the Holy Spirit "nesting" in me! Do you?

The other image of a dove is, of course, found in the story of Noah in Genesis. It was a dove that was sent out to see if the flood waters had receded, coming back a second time with a green leaf which showed that trees were now exposed and living. The dove carries with it the hope of new life.

I mentioned earlier that everything Jesus did, He did through the power of the Holy Spirit. This is why He needed the baptism of the Holy Spirit. When Jesus came to earth as a baby and grew into a man, He chose to limit Himself to what it means to be human. He laid aside some of His divine attributes. Things like being able to be everywhere at the same time – His omnipresence. He also laid aside His knowing everything. We see Him asking questions to people such as, "Who touched me?" He spoke of the second coming, but said that even He didn't know the actual time for it – "only the Father knows" (Matthew 24:36). Instead He put on the cloak of humanity, embracing every aspect of what it is to be fully human.

Jesus was completely reliant on His Father knowing everything. He needed the empowering of the Holy Spirit to fulfil His Father's will. Before His baptism in water, when He was also anointed from heaven, Jesus performed no miracles and had not healed anyone. He wanted to show us that this is what we need to live a life of fullness on earth. If He had been the only person to ever do miracles there would have been no point. Jesus showed us what happens when we invite the Holy Spirit to fill us, as He experienced.

THE GIFT

> *On one occasion, while he was eating with them, he gave them this command: "Do not leave Jerusalem, but wait for the gift my Father promised, which you have heard me speak about..."*
>
> **Acts 1:4**

Jesus told the disciples to wait for the *gift*. A gift is usually something that gives us pleasure, something given freely that costs the receiver nothing.

The important thing here is that a gift needs to be *received*, otherwise the purpose of it is redundant. Think of someone giving you a huge box filled with diamonds. Your body language and everything about you should reflect an attitude of receiving, not grabbing. To receive a gift well, there needs to be humility, thankfulness, wonder and joy.

The disciples were told to wait for an amazing gift that Jesus described as "power from on high" (Luke 24:49). This must have raised their levels of expectation and anticipation a fair amount!

What would this gift be like? What would happen once they were given it? Would it be theirs for ever?

THE WATER

Jesus said:

> *Let anyone who is thirsty come to me and drink. Whoever*
> *believes in me, as Scripture has said, rivers of living water*
> *will flow from within them.*

John 7:37–38

Even before we invite the Holy Spirit to come and fill us, we discover Jesus has invited us already!

Jesus told the woman at the well that if she drank the water of the Holy Spirit she would never be thirsty again. When we are dry we have a drink. It quenches our thirst and revitalizes us. Without water we would die. Jesus gave an invitation to whoever is spiritually thirsty, knowing that without Him, we will die.

Like water, His Holy Spirit refreshes us, cleanses us, revives us.

THE WIND

The wind is an image sometimes used in the Bible to describe the presence of God. In John chapter 3 Jesus tells Nicodemus that:

> *The wind blows wherever it pleases. You hear its sound, but*
> *you cannot tell where it comes from or where it is going. So*
> *it is with everyone born of the Spirit.*

John 3:8

The wind that blew in the upper room at Pentecost was the wind from heaven. The disciples could not see it, but they could hear it. If you imagine a violent wind blowing, what usually happens is that it shakes anything in its path.

The Holy Spirit will sometimes do that with us. He shakes us up to awaken us or cause things to fall off us that have stuck to us. Think of autumn when the leaves change colour and die. The wind comes and blows them away, leaving the tree ready for new growth in the spring. Sometimes, people shake in the Holy Spirit for the same reason. God is loosing them up from the old to prepare them for the new.

THE FIRE

Following on from the wind, the disciples saw tongues of fire that separated and came to rest on them. Fire is hot and it burns. Symbolically it would seem that an anointing was taking place and they were being set apart for a purpose. They were being empowered, energized for what was to come.

Elsewhere in the Bible we read that gold and silver are purged of impurities by being placed in fire. God will allow us to experience a *refiner's fire* which, although often a testing time, leads to purification.

> *In all this you greatly rejoice, though now for a little while you may have had to suffer grief in all kinds of trials. These have come so that the proven genuineness of your faith – of greater worth than gold, which perishes even though refined by fire – may result in praise, glory and honor when Jesus Christ is revealed.*
>
> **1 Peter 1:6–7**

THE LANGUAGE

I am devoting a whole chapter later in the book to the gift of tongues, but it is worthy of mention here. The presence of the Holy Spirit was shown by the sudden release of different languages the disciples had never spoken before.

At the time of Pentecost, Jerusalem was awash with

representatives from many different nations and cultures. These people came running when they heard their language being spoken by the disciples. Imagine you were in a country where no one spoke your language, and suddenly you heard familiar words and phrases. You would be curious and drawn to the person or people, although it would be slightly bewildering.

It was decided by those listening that the disciples were drunk, as the Holy Spirit was causing them to do things that drunken people would normally do. Many of the disciples could not stand up properly under the power of the Holy Spirit.

You may already have seen people act like this when the Holy Spirit has come into a meeting you were in. It may have made you anxious or a bit unsure. You may have felt excluded or inferior. Most, if not all, of these feelings will be because we don't understand how the Holy Spirit works. He does not mind if we feel unsure. We must not let our lack of understanding get in the way of what He might want to do in and through us.

PRAYER

Dear Holy Spirit, You know that I get worried about what You might do, in me and through me. I realize I will never be able to understand You with my mind or work You out. I choose to give You now all my fears about being filled with You. I give You the fear that I will be out of control. I trust You with control of my life. I want to know more of the presence of Jesus. I want to be filled to overflowing with You so that I will be bold like the disciples were. Amen.

ACTION

Now seems like a good time to pause and think about these things.

The Holy Spirit is a part of God and He will not act outside of what we know about God from the Bible. We know that God is loving, totally good, kind, patient, gracious and forgiving. We know that He is our Shepherd who leads us into all truth, never harming us, but always protecting us.

Will you trust the Holy Spirit to be gentle with you?

Can you be honest with Him about your fears or feelings of inadequacy?

The Bible tells us to not simply be filled with the Holy Spirit, but to *keep on being filled*. Why? As my vicar, David Pytches, used to say, "Because we leak!" As we draw from the pool of living water, we need daily refilling. Otherwise we will become dry and operate out of our "flesh" – our own inadequate strength.

So are you ready for an adventure?

THE GOOD NEWS

You can be filled with the Holy Spirit wherever you are! You do not have to be in a church or a traditional "holy place"; there are no geographical boundaries or restrictions with the Holy Spirit.

As I mentioned earlier, you may ask now to be filled, but it may not happen immediately; it may be within hours or days. The important thing to remember is that when we ask, God is not deaf; He hears us and He will answer. He wants us to be filled with the Holy Spirit. We don't have to persuade Him or worry that He may forget. The important thing is to be in an attitude of receiving.

You can do the next part either alone or with a friend or in a group. Or you can ask someone who has experienced the baptism of the Holy Spirit to lay hands on you to pray that you are filled with the Holy Spirit too.

TAKE YOUR TIME – THERE'S NO NEED TO RUSH

Take this next section step by step. Allow the Holy Spirit time to minister to you without worrying about silences, because He doesn't mind silence! He will come to you, so you can be peaceful and relaxed.

Stand or sit and begin to pray...

Be clean

Jesus, I want to be a clean place for the Holy Spirit.
I ask that You would show me anything I need
cleansing from, so that He can feel welcome.

Let Jesus show you anything that you need to repent (turn away) from. If something comes to mind, confess it. Be honest with Jesus about it and don't try to ignore it. If it comes to your mind, then Jesus wants to set you free from the effect it is having on you. Receive the forgiveness that Jesus is offering you and thank Him. Remember that the blood of Jesus Christ, God's Son, cleanses us from all sin (1 John 1:9).

now Receive

Now be in an attitude of receiving. I usually ask people to open up their hands in front of them as if they were about to receive a gift. Now pray:

Please come, Holy Spirit. I invite You to fill me so that
I overflow with You. I receive You now.

And wait...

The Holy Spirit has heard you, so you only need to wait now. You might not feel anything, see anything or hear anything, but that is OK. He will meet you His way because He knows what you need.

Breathe in the Holy Spirit and breathe out everything else.

Be conscious of Jesus and how wonderful He is, how much

you love Him and how much He has done for you.

If someone else is laying hands on you, they can invite the Holy Spirit into your mind, body and soul (including your emotions).

Drink Him in. Let Him flow into you and through you. Invite streams of living water to flow into you and up out of you.

WIND AND FIRE

Invite the wind of the Holy Spirit to blow away anything that doesn't belong, anything that clings to you that is unhelpful.

Invite the Holy Spirit to come upon you as fire, to purge out impurities and to burn in you passion and boldness for Jesus.

Thank you, Lord. You do it – You fill me now.

BE COMFORTABLE

As you continue to receive from the Holy Spirit you may want to relax and lie on the floor. If you are standing you may want to sit, especially if you are worried about falling over!

The most important thing right now is that you give time to let the Holy Spirit wash over you and fill you up. Keep drinking in the love of God, engaging your mind with thoughts of Jesus.

Remember, this is not to test how spiritual you are compared to everyone else.

Just be you.

THANK YOU

When you are ready, say thank you to Jesus. He has heard your prayers and answered them by sending His Holy Spirit to fill you to overflowing.

Isn't that wonderful?

CHAPTER 4

WHY DO PEOPLE FALL AND SHAKE?

There is a danger in writing a chapter about this subject because some people may accuse me of not supporting my claims with Scripture. Some of the manifestations of the Holy Spirit are not easy to explain or understand. To try and put principles around it in order to prove a point simply will not work, as the Holy Spirit's activity is not confined to my principles! He can and will do whatever He wants to.

However, I did not want to avoid this subject because many people are so concerned and worried about the effects and manifestations of the Spirit that they back away, wanting nothing more to do with Him. That is a tragedy. My aim, therefore, is to provide some encouragement with stories from Scripture and testimonies from my own life and the lives of others.

FALLING OVER IS IN THE BIBLE!

There are a number of instances in the Bible where people fell to the floor when they were profoundly aware of the presence of God or when they received a message from Him through an angelic visitation. Look at this example in the book of Daniel:

So I was left alone, gazing at this great vision; I had no strength left, my face turned deathly pale and I was helpless. Then I heard him speaking, and as I listened to him, I fell into a deep sleep, my face to the ground.

A hand touched me and set me trembling on my hands and knees. He said, "Daniel, you who are highly esteemed, consider carefully the words I am about to speak to you, and stand up, for I have now been sent to you." And when he said this to me, I stood up trembling.

Daniel 10:8–11

At the dedication of the temple, Scripture states that the priests could not perform their duties because the glory of the Lord filled the temple of God and they could not continue to blow their trumpets. The context implies that they were overcome by the Holy Spirit:

Then the temple of the Lord was filled with the cloud, and the priests could not perform their service because of the cloud, for the glory of the Lord filled the temple of God.

2 Chronicles 5:13–14

In Gethsemane, when Jesus was arrested, the soldiers fell to the ground when He stated, "I am He" in response to their searching for Jesus the Nazarene (John 18:4–6).

So too for Paul on the road to Damascus:

As he neared Damascus on his journey, suddenly a light from heaven flashed around him. He fell to the ground and heard a voice say to him, "Saul, Saul, why do you persecute me?"

Acts 9:3–4

You may want to search a concordance for yourself or look online at www.biblegateway.com, putting "fell to the ground" into the search box and seeing what it reveals. Sometimes we can criticize out of ignorance and lack of knowledge, rather than because we believe something is actually ungodly. It is important we learn before we judge.

So falling over in the presence of God is not a new phenomenon.

Through the centuries the Holy Spirit has operated in this way. There are many historical accounts available for us to read of how the Holy Spirit came on people in power and they fell to the ground as a result.

WHY FALLING?

Sometimes, the Holy Spirit wants to move us from a standing to a lying position because He wants us to rest or "soak" in His presence, or possibly to gently lead us to relinquish control, so that He can do a deep work of deliverance or healing there and then. It happens most often during prayer ministry, but can happen during worship when the Holy Spirit is moving.

WHAT IS IT LIKE TO FALL OVER IN THE HOLY SPIRIT?

Some people experience their legs feeling weak and they find they can no longer stand up properly. Others become overwhelmed by their love for Jesus and their bodies respond to this by no longer being able to support them. Often, when the peace of the Holy Spirit descends, it just feels good to relax back into a chair without the need to go all the way down to the floor.

The Holy Spirit loves to heal us and can do His work more fully when we are in a relaxed state. For some people, it seems as if they are receiving an anaesthetic before some spiritual healing surgery while lying on the floor. At times they don't even know what happened, but later, once they are standing up again, they feel as if something was removed that had been oppressing or troubling them. For others, during this relaxed state, God shows them something from their history that they have not grieved over or resolved. During this time there can be big expressions of grief or a release of crying, or even moaning, screaming or shouting. It can sound a bit scary to an onlooker, but it really is a wonderful thing for someone to release pain that has been locked away for years.

I have been present when someone has been resting in the Holy Spirit on the floor and has experienced deliverance and deep inner healing. At other times, people have told me they have received a specific revelation from Jesus or had a deep, life-changing encounter. In my twenty-five years of ministering to people at church services or at conferences and festivals, I have never heard of anyone who has genuinely rested in the Spirit where it has not ended up being a positive experience.

I have seen people lie on the floor for an hour or more when, for them, it feels like just five minutes. There have been times when someone who had been involved in devil worship and other occult practices received full deliverance after falling over in the Spirit – afterwards remembering nothing of what happened. After opening their eyes and standing up in complete peace, they could remember falling to the floor but nothing of what followed as they were delivered. Isn't God wonderful? I believe it is His love and grace that puts them into a deep sleep while He performs His "surgery".

DO PEOPLE GET HURT WHEN THEY FALL OVER?

There may be concern that a person could get hurt through falling over. When it has been a genuine encounter with the Holy Spirit, I have never seen anyone hurt from falling to the ground.

I remember an instance in South Africa when my husband was praying for someone. As this man fell under the power of the Holy Spirit he landed on a chair that broke into about four pieces! But the man felt nothing and had no idea, as he "rested" on the floor with the Lord, that others were standing with mouths open wide at the destruction of the chair!

How can this happen? I don't know, but there are a lot of things I don't understand in encounters with God.

DO I HAVE TO FALL OVER?

Of course, we don't have to fall to the ground for the Lord to heal us of something. It is not a rule and we should be careful that we do not put any experience on a pedestal.

However, the key thing is that we hold it in balance. Just as we should not fake it and be fleshly in our falling over, neither should we resist it. When the Holy Spirit comes upon us, we have the choice to either go with what is happening or not. On occasions I have prayed for someone and seen them resisting the overwhelming love and power of the Holy Spirit because they are afraid of falling. In this instance I usually suggest that they might like to sit on the floor or a chair, or lie down so that they can feel more relaxed about receiving.

Fear can keep us from the full blessing that the Holy Spirit wants to pour into our lives. Abandoning ourselves to Him, whether we fall over or not, is more important than anything else.

WHAT IF I'M THE ONE PRAYING FOR PEOPLE?

It can feel like a big responsibility if someone falls over after we have prayed for them. In reality, the interaction between the Holy Spirit and the person on the floor or chair is really where the good stuff is, so just be wise and don't get in the way.

However, it is always a good idea to stay with someone if they are "resting in the Spirit" (or, as our pastor calls it, "assuming the horizontal"!), and sit them up slowly afterwards. Sometimes the Holy Spirit is still resting on them and they are not in full charge of their own legs for a while. If you are praying for many people, it is helpful to return back to those on the floor from time to time.

There is no status to be gained from the fact that you can pray and see people fall over sometimes. In the same way, there is no status if you yourself have fallen over. We don't want to get into a habit of expecting people to fall over, nor take any credit to ourselves if people do fall. It is the Lord who overwhelms them and He must have the glory!

HOW not to DO It

Unfortunately, there have been instances on TV where people seem to have been pushed over – almost as if the minister feels this must happen to verify their ministry. It is distasteful to watch and serves no purpose other than putting people off ever receiving hands-on ministry. We also should never hit people, punch them or push them in any way!

This may sound obvious, but believe me, I have heard of many bizarre practices which do not honour God or the people being ministered to. I am sad to say that my husband and I have also witnessed members of a ministry team pushing people over. I remember one particular instance, many years ago, when we were at a well-known Christian festival. The previous day, some basic training had been given to a small group of willing volunteers who subsequently joined the existing prayer ministry team. The following day they received a "red spot" on their badge to show that they were authorized to be on the team. To our horror, we saw one of them hit someone in the stomach while ministering healing. My husband was given the job of "de-spotting" the person until they had the opportunity for more training!

The Holy Spirit will never be violent with people. I remember reading a book once about a man I will call Jim, who became a Christian while in prison. He had previously led a gangster-type lifestyle, but was now transformed – well, almost! One day Jim was kneeling in his cell praying when another inmate came in, mocking him for praying. Jim wasted no time in head-butting this man who, under the force of it, fell to the ground. As he came round, the man said to Jim, "Blimey, if it means that much to you, there must be something in it." He then knelt down, asking Jesus into his life! A week later Jim did exactly the same thing with a different inmate, and he too became a Christian. As I read this I was shocked and thought that this method of ministry was extremely odd – until I read the next line, which said, "... and then God showed me a better way!"

Sometimes we do hear of healing following bizarre practices. This does not necessarily mean that what the person did was good or right. What it means is that God can heal people despite how much we muck it up!

SHƏKIN6

Just as falling over is not new, shaking in the power of the Holy Spirit can be traced back through the centuries.

The Quakers, a movement that began in England in the seventeenth century, were originally so called because during their meetings people would "quake" or shake under the power of the Holy Spirit.

WHY DOES SHƏKIN6 HƏPPEN?

Sometimes when I see people shaking a lot, I get a sense that Jesus is shaking something off them – freeing them. However, if this goes on for too long, people just get exhausted. We have to be careful that we don't get caught up in the manifestation and preoccupied by the shaking itself.

Shaking can be a sign that the Holy Spirit is engaged in healing, imparting a spiritual gift, anointing through empowering or setting a person apart for a particular purpose.

It is worth remembering, regarding the Holy Spirit's anointing, that shaking may only be the start of a time of preparation. Just because they are shaking does not mean they are ready to walk immediately in what God has set them apart for. Even Jesus was led by the Holy Spirit into the wilderness for a time of severe testing before He became engaged in the ministry to which His Father had called Him.

SHAKING CAN BE CONTAGIOUS

I remember once watching someone in our church shaking as he sat listening to the sermon. The top part of his body began rippling while his lower half remained completely still. After watching him for a while, the Holy Spirit suddenly came upon me in a powerful way. Sometimes the Holy Spirit is "catching" – so watch out!

Similar to falling over in the Spirit, we do not have to shake for the Holy Spirit to be doing something powerful in us. But when we start to sense His power on us, we have a choice. We can either go with what is happening or choose to opt out. Ironically, sometimes when the Holy Spirit is upon us powerfully, and we try to stop what is happening, it can result in the power manifesting even more!

I remember when I first started to minister to people, I didn't know what to do with my hands because they used to shake. We were encouraged by our pastor, David Pytches, to lay both hands on people so that they wouldn't move about too much, as others watching the ministry might find this off-putting and weird. Willing to comply, I did this, only to discover that my legs shook instead! Fortunately, no one seemed to notice this, so I was very relieved!

WE ALL RESPOND DIFFERENTLY

Experiencing the manifestations of the Holy Spirit is often due to the fact that God is dealing with us in some way. Sometimes it is simply our response to His presence and power. However we manifest in the Holy Spirit, we will all respond differently because we are all different.

Be careful of getting into bad habits. Sometimes, what starts off being God ends up with us! In our desire to replicate our previous encounters, we think we should help God along a little bit. This is immaturity. Although we are encouraged in

Scripture to be like little children, it does not mean that we give way to unwise behaviour that is not of the Spirit. Let Him do His work in you, His way.

It Can Be Bizarre at Times!

The Holy Spirit is not a performer and He will not do things just to shock us or to draw attention to Himself. We may not be able to explain some of the more extreme manifestations of His presence, but we can guarantee that if it is Him and not someone acting in a fleshly way, He has a purpose for it.

One of the most unusual examples I have ever witnessed was someone under the power of the Holy Spirit swimming backstroke (without water) across an entire auditorium! Personally, I have fallen to the floor, sliding off a chair in slow motion, looking a bit like a silk scarf. I have also experienced the whole of my body bouncing on the floor, lifting up some six centimetres. On another occasion, whilst I was receiving healing for my neck which I had injured in an accident, my body contorted into the shape of a corkscrew. This was observed by a doctor who said afterwards that the human body cannot do what I had just done! Following this, I could lift both my arms up in the air for the first time since my accident.

So why does God do these things? Why doesn't He do it in a less embarrassing way? The short answer to this is, we do not know, but we know He is good all the time and He loves us.

These experiences do not make us more spiritual and, in my own experience, they did not make me feel any closer to God. But I certainly felt more hungry for Him. I remember telling Him that however exciting they were, I did not want all these experiences at the cost of knowing *Him*.

SOME OTHER MANIFESTATIONS

I want to list a few other examples of what happens to people when the Holy Spirit is present in power.

WEEPING

Once when I prayed for a man I will call Greg, he began to receive the Holy Spirit's anointing. Tears started to stream down his face and his body began to gently shake. I sensed Jesus was imparting to Greg His compassion for broken people and I had a picture of him with people of different races. The manifestations of both weeping and shaking increased under the anointing of the Holy Spirit and later I asked him what had happened. He explained that his job had been as a court prosecutor, but after sustaining a head injury in an accident he had to resign. Just before his accident the Lord had been speaking to him about the young men he had been prosecuting – that they were offending because of the impact of their troubled backgrounds.

During the prayer time he had seen a pair of red eyes and many young black teens wearing chains. He saw himself breaking their chains and setting them free. There were no more angry red eyes to haunt them. As he wept, Greg knew that God was renaming him "liberator" instead of "prosecutor"!

A SENSE OF PEACE

Most of us have experienced a sense of peace during a time of waiting on the Lord – during a prayer time, for instance. This too is a manifestation of the Holy Spirit. For some of us this can seem more acceptable, as it has no obvious, visible sign to those watching. Jesus said He was leaving us with His peace, so we should not always expect the manifestations of the Holy Spirit to be noisy.

BLINDING

Although unusual, being temporarily "blinded" in the Holy Spirit can also be a mark of His presence.

I have not personally come across this happening to anyone over a long period of time, but I have known people who are resting in the Spirit say that they cannot open their eyes. When this has happened they are not usually frightened at all, but feel complete peace. Sometimes their eyes are moving beneath their lids as if they are seeing something. Later they testify to seeing visions or things being revealed to them that Jesus wanted to heal or set them free from.

As I mentioned earlier in the chapter, this also happened to the apostle Paul on the road to Damascus in Acts chapter 9.

BEING STRUCK DUMB

Another unusual manifestation of the Holy Spirit is being struck dumb. In Luke's gospel we read about Zechariah, married to Elizabeth, who was struck dumb when an angel appeared to him foretelling the birth of John the Baptist. The angel told him that since Zechariah didn't believe the words that were prophesied, he would remain dumb until the prophecy was fulfilled.

On one occasion, to the delight of my husband, I was struck dumb for a short time! It happened this way:

I had been in a service at our church when there had been another outpouring of the Holy Spirit. I was so overwhelmed by the magnificence of Jesus that in amongst it all I felt a "filling" of my mouth. I remember being so in awe of God and drove home still in the same attitude. I felt that in the holiness of His presence in and around me, I couldn't speak and neither did I want to. So I crept upstairs and lay on my bed. My husband came up to see where I was, and I signed with my hand that he should leave me and smiled at him. There followed the most incredible time where I heard angels singing and I was caught up in wonderful adoration of Jesus. It lasted for a few hours. I hardly slept at all that night, but felt refreshed in the morning. When I explained to my husband what had happened, he encouraged me to go with whatever was happening, as he had had the quietest evening in a long time!

LAUGHTER

Laughter can be God given. Holy Spirit laughter is releasing, refreshing, healing and a great stress reliever. I have been in gatherings where Holy Spirit laughter broke out in one corner of the auditorium and then spread throughout the building. At other times, I have seen laughter break out simultaneously in different parts of the room.

Most often, people do not know what they are laughing about!

I remember a time at a John Wimber conference when the Holy Spirit fell on the whole auditorium with a Spirit of repentance. People were crying and wailing in repentance for about an hour. After this there was a break for coffee. When we reassembled John started to read from 1 Corinthians chapter 13, the famous passage about love. As he was speaking I happened to look down and saw a man dressed in a raincoat resting in the Spirit. To everyone else this man didn't look in the least bit comical, but as I looked at him the Holy Spirit came upon me mightily, causing me to burst out laughing. I tried to stop myself with both hands over my mouth, but this caused me to laugh even louder. It was as if the laughter had a power and energy of its own. It seemed like it was pushing itself through my fingers and couldn't be stopped. I wanted the floor to open up and swallow me whole, as it seemed so disrespectful to the speaker and the Lord, as Scripture was being read.

By this time half of me was mortified while the other half was letting rip with excessive laughter, and I had by now half fallen off my chair! John Wimber took his glasses off and gave me the longest stare. He shut the Bible and said, "The Lord is here. He is having a party tonight." By this time the laughter was spreading at a rapid rate around the room. It was raucous. For as long as we had cried earlier, we were now laughing hysterically. For hours afterwards our stomachs ached as our muscles had had a full work-out. During the time of repentance many people had received visions and prophetic words that were life changing. This happened many years ago, but it is engraved in my memory as being a very significant time.

I have also been present when laughter is spilling out in different parts of the room and I have been totally unaffected by it. At these times I have smiled and enjoyed seeing others receiving. I know that some people long for this to happen to them because they want to experience something that looks such good fun. Unfortunately, this isn't something that we can choose or make happen. It is a manifestation of the Holy Spirit and He chooses how and when it happens. Let us just join in by blessing what God is doing when He chooses to do it.

BIRtHING

Finally, there is the Holy Spirit manifestation of giving birth.

This happened to me once while I was stretched out on a church pew. It can look and sound very bizarre, like the person is having contractions. The good news is, unlike the real thing, this doesn't hurt!

When it happens there can be a powerful compulsion to "bear down", but in my case it all happened in my throat. The sounds being emitted sounded just like a woman in labour. I have seen both men and women doing this.

Why does this happen, and to whom? I believe that, spiritually speaking, people are giving birth to new ministries or new happenings in their life. Personally, I had dreams of holding newborn babies for a period of two years before first having this "birthing" manifestation. In all, I have probably given birth spiritually six times. Each time this has resulted in a massive change in what I have been doing in ministry. I have spoken to other people after they have had such an experience and they all knew that either God had shown them what they were being called into during this birth experience, or it was the crowning act after months of being shown by God what was ahead.

A FINAL WORD

The danger in sharing these things is that this may be seen as evidence of pride. The truth is, I do not know why Jesus has allowed me to experience so many manifestations of the Holy Spirit over the years. All I know is that in them, I have received times of deep healing, which have been sometimes painful. At other times I have been refreshed, empowered, freed and blessed. I know it may have looked strange to the onlooker at times, but all I can say to that is that I know I have always been in safe hands. As far as I am concerned, this is what I should expect from an all-powerful God who made the world, raises the dead and heals people!

I first became a Christian at St Andrews Church, Chorleywood and at that point I gave permission to the Holy Spirit to have free reign in my life. Many years later, when we helped Mike Pilavachi start Soul Survivor Watford Church, I started to quench the Holy Spirit. I was conscious of the fact that most of the congregation were young, impressionable people. I did not want anything God might want to do in me to get in the way of them receiving from Jesus for themselves. Since some of the manifestations might have appeared a bit weird, I actually stopped receiving from the Holy Spirit rather than go with what He was doing.

A few years ago I saw what I had done and repented of it. In retrospect, I wish I had not repressed what the Holy Spirit wanted to do in me. Remember that God wants to use you and me as catalysts for His power.

Let's stay open to Him!

PRAYER

Jesus, I want to receive more from You. Thank You that I am safe with You. I don't want to limit what You may want to do in me. I choose to give over control to You. Free me from fear of what You might do or how You will do it. I lay down before You any need to experience manifestations as proof to me that You are real. I want You to take my concerns about what I will look like, sound like or act like when Your Holy Spirit falls on me. Free me to be the person You created me to be. I do not want to pursue these things at the cost of pursuing You, but ask You to lead me so that You become more and more real to me in the years ahead. Amen.

ACTION

The manifestations of the Holy Spirit are not a new invention. They did not start at the same time as the charismatic movement! God will sometimes connect with people by His Holy Spirit in physical ways. Don't fear it – embrace it.

Is there anything you are scared about receiving from the Holy Spirit?

Would you like to be released in freedom to receive whatever He has for you?

Would you like to surrender control of your life to the Holy Spirit now?

SCRIPTURES

When Jesus said, "I am he," they drew back and fell to the ground.

John 18:6

*As he neared Damascus on his journey, suddenly a light
from heaven flashed around him. He fell to the ground and
heard a voice say to him, "Saul, Saul, why do you persecute
me?"*

"Who are you, Lord?" Saul asked.

*"I am Jesus, whom you are persecuting," he replied.
"Now get up and go into the city, and you will be told what
you must do."*

Acts 9:3–6

*After they prayed, the place where they were meeting was
shaken. And they were all filled with the Holy Spirit and
spoke the word of God boldly.*

Acts 4:31

*The hand of the Lord was on me there, and he said to me,
"Get up and go out to the plain, and there I will speak to
you." So I got up and went out to the plain. And the glory of
the Lord was standing there, like the glory I had seen by the
Kebar River, and I fell facedown.*

Then the Spirit came into me and raised me to my feet.

Ezekiel 3:22–24

*My heart is broken within me; all my bones tremble. I am
like a drunken man, like a strong man overcome by wine,
because of the Lord and his holy words.*

Jeremiah 23:9

CHAPTER 5

GIFTS OF THE HOLY SPIRIT

God is very generous to us. He gives us gifts to show us how much He loves us, equipping us for everything He wants us to be. We must never forget that Jesus and the Holy Spirit are God's gifts to us.

For God so loved the world that he gave his one and only Son, that whoever believes in him shall not perish but have eternal life.

John 3:16

But when Jesus was preparing His disciples for His departure back to heaven, He encouraged them and showed them how they would shortly be equipped for service:

And I will ask the Father, and he will give you another advocate to help you and be with you forever – the Spirit of truth. The world cannot accept him, because it neither sees him nor knows him. But you know him, for he lives with you and will be in you.

John 14:16–17

God never intended to leave us alone when Jesus went back to His Father. Instead, He gave us His Holy Spirit and we are told to eagerly desire His gifts (1 Corinthians 14:1). In other words, we can actually *ask* Him to give us specific gifts so that we can be a blessing to the people we meet.

Now to each one the manifestation of the Spirit is given for the common good.

1 Corinthians 12:7

SO WHAT ARE SPIRITUAL GIFTS?

The gifts of the Holy Spirit are spiritual *tools* to be used both for the building up of the church and for those outside of the church, to extend the kingdom of God.

These spiritual tools are not like trophies or badges given for achievements to accumulate and admire. They are love gifts from God and should be used for His glory. Some of the gifts we can read about in the New Testament are in the following passage:

To one there is given through the Spirit a message of wisdom, to another a message of knowledge by means of the same Spirit, to another faith by the same Spirit, to another gifts of healing by that one Spirit, to another miraculous powers, to another prophecy, to another distinguishing between spirits, to another speaking in different kinds of tongues, and to still another the interpretation of tongues. All these are the work of one and the same Spirit, and he distributes them to each one, just as he determines.

1 Corinthians 12:8–11

In Paul's letter to the Romans, we read that the Holy Spirit gives the gifts of *prophecy*, *serving*, *teaching*, *encouragement*, *giving*, *leading* and *mercy* (Romans 12:3–8). Also, *celibacy* is a gift of the Holy Spirit (1 Corinthians 7:7–8), as are *philanthropy* (1 Corinthians 13:3) and *hospitality* (1 Peter 4:9).

73

MY AIM

To examine every one of these gifts in greater detail you would need to read a much thicker book than this one. In my introduction, "What Is This Book About?" I wrote that my aim was to make this book as practical as possible. In this chapter I will give a general overview of the gifts of the Holy Spirit, drawing attention to some in particular. In the chapters that follow, we will explore some of them in greater detail and you will read some stories from my own experience. My hope is that it will encourage you to be bold and ask God for them – and then try them out!

If you would like to find out more about the gifts I will not be writing about, look up each one online, putting the title of a particular gift in the search engine, and see what you find. That may be enough for you, but if you want to take it further and do some Bible study of your own, there are websites for that too.

THEY ARE ALL WORTH HAVING!

Certain spiritual gifts may sound really exciting and appealing, while others are easier to ignore because they function better "behind the scenes". Some of the dramatic gifts like prophecy, words of knowledge and miracles seem more like "power tools", while others, like the gifts of encouragement, serving, administration and mercy are more like "spiritual muscles" within the church: necessary, but mainly hidden.

The church is described in the Bible as the body of Christ, which is made up of many parts. The parts described are like organs and limbs. Without muscles, a body cannot move its bones or its limbs. Spiritual muscles also need to be exercised and used; otherwise, just like our human bodies, the "body" (the church) will end up floppy and flabby.

Remember that *all* of the gifts are important and *all* of them are supernatural. Don't get caught in the trap of believing that some are more attractive than others. The church would be unbalanced if everyone prophesied but no one was hospitable! This would be a really bad witness to unbelievers. So each gift is important and they should all be fully functioning in the church to help it grow.

My husband and I are almost "past our sell-by date", so we have started going to the gym twice a week! Muscles that I did not even know I had have started to stretch and grow. Even walking up the stairs has become easier. I feel more energetic in the mornings than I have done for years. How much more will using all the gifts of the Holy Spirit accomplish God's purposes inside and outside of the church.

THE GIFT OF ENCOURAGEMENT

This is a great gift to ask for. We are all meant to naturally encourage one another, but a supernatural gift of encouragement is a much deeper thing and can change people's lives for the better. It is not flattery, as flattery is fake and the Bible warns us to steer clear of it. God-given encouragement is like water to the soul. One of the best ways to illustrate how it operates it is to tell you about someone who has it.

Before he retired, David Pytches was our vicar and pastor while we were at St Andrews, Chorleywood. He is well known as someone who exercises the gift of encouragement with people he meets.

In those days I was always bursting with new ideas, particularly in the area of "bridge building" into our local community. I would want to share my ideas with David in order to be accountable and see whether my ideas were viable. When I would tell David what I was thinking, he would always listen carefully and then give me a specific word of encouragement. Each time the word would penetrate my heart, changing what was just an embryonic idea in my head into fuel for action. I would leave our meeting with passion and excitement rising up inside me. I would feel energized and full of hope, grateful for the freedom to dream and to grow as the Holy Spirit led. It was wonderful to know that through David's gift of encouragement, I could hear that God was cheering me on.

> *Joseph, a Levite from Cyprus, whom the apostles called*
> *Barnabas (which means "son of encouragement")...*
>
> **Acts 4:36**

In the New Testament, one of the believers was nicknamed Barnabas, which meant "Son of Encouragement", because he often displayed this gift. He sold a field he owned, giving the proceeds to his leaders. Barnabas was the one who encouraged the Christians who feared Saul that his conversion on the road to Damascus was authentic, so they need fear him no more.

> *When he came to Jerusalem, he tried to join the disciples,*
> *but they were all afraid of him, not believing that he really*
> *was a disciple. But Barnabas took him and brought him*
> *to the apostles. He told them how Saul on his journey had*
> *seen the Lord and that the Lord had spoken to him, and how*
> *in Damascus he had preached fearlessly in the name of*
> *Jesus. So Saul stayed with them and moved about freely in*
> *Jerusalem, speaking boldly in the name of the Lord.*
>
> **Acts 9:26–28**

THE GIFT OF HOSPITALITY

People who operate in this gift may not realize that it is a supernatural gift. They are probably people who naturally gather other people into their home, wanting them to feel welcomed and comfortable. It is a gift to be treasured in a church because when new people join, the main reason they stay is usually related to how welcome they are made to feel. Recently, I heard of a young woman who had visited a church five times, and on each occasion not one person spoke to her. What a shame! People are looking for meaningful relationships. It is essential that the body of Christ is a place where they thrive.

Ruth, one of our pastors at Soul Survivor, has this particular gift. Each week she will buy loads of food because she spontaneously invites people round for a meal all the time. She likes nothing better than to spend time making people feel welcome in her home. Ruth is a gatherer of people across the spectrum of age, ability and status, and she makes them all feel special.

Another of our pastors, Dave, is always getting people together for a fun activity. He can transform an area that looks bare and unwelcoming into a space that is both a delight to the eyes and also has the elements for making someone feel special. Dave's home is also always full of people. With his wife, Jane, he has recently planted a church for young families. This is bound to be successful because Dave's gift of hospitality is constantly being released throughout the area where they live.

I believe that Martha (whose name actually means "mistress of the house") in the gospels had the gift of hospitality. She and her sister Mary were always welcoming people into their home.

If you think you have this gift, why not get together with others who are like minded in your church and think of creative ways you can use it both inside the church and outside it.

THE GIFT OF DISCERNING OF SPIRITS

This may sound a bit odd to you. What does it mean? Unlike natural discernment and even common sense, this gift functions in the supernatural realm. The Bible says that Jesus, who lived and ministered in the anointing of the Holy Spirit, knew what people were like and what motives lay behind their words and actions. John's gospel tells us:

He did not need any testimony about mankind, for he knew what was in each person.

John 2:25

People who have this gift of the Holy Spirit can look at someone and know what spiritual forces are motivating them. Just as we can be filled with the Holy Spirit, some people can be manipulated by evil spirits or controlled by fleshly desires. It is good that God gives this gift to His church, since the enemy will often seek to counterfeit spiritual gifts, hoping to place his agents in key positions in the church and society. The gift of discernment will pick this up immediately.

In the Bible we read that people called out to Jesus or the disciples, saying something that in itself was true (Mark 1:21–28, 5:1–13; Luke 4:41). However, just because it was a true statement did not mean it came from a pure source. The enemy would use people like this to act as a distraction, an irritation to the work of God and the advancement of His kingdom.

In Acts we can read a story that illustrates how this happened to the disciples. Paul and Silas had travelled to Philippi, meeting a businesswoman called Lydia, who accepted Jesus as her Saviour. Her whole family were then saved and a new church plant was started in that place. The enemy then used a slave girl to disrupt things, but because Paul operated in the gift of discernment, he did not succeed:

Once when we were going to the place of prayer, we were met by a female slave who had a spirit by which she predicted the future. She earned a great deal of money for her owners by fortune-telling. She followed Paul and the rest of us, shouting, "These men are servants of the Most High God, who are telling you the way to be saved." She kept this up for many days. Finally Paul became so annoyed that he turned around and said to the spirit, "In the name of Jesus Christ I command you to come out of her!" At that moment the spirit left her.

Acts 16:16–18

Jesus often confronted people who, with their mouths, sounded pious, but actually their words came from either a sinful heart or an evil spirit speaking out of them.

THE GIFT OF GIVING

If you receive something from a person with this gift, then you can feel like you have been given something from God Himself. Wonderful!

This gift can be defined as giving to the needs of others without counting the cost. It can also mean the giving of ourselves wholly to a task or situation.

Often people with this gift are excellent financial stewards and will use it by offering themselves as a treasurer for a church or charity, or involve themselves in debt counselling, perhaps running courses in how to manage personal finance and so on.

People with this gift are often trusted by God to enter the high-earning bracket, generating vast wealth from their business dealings. This means that they then give their money to whomever the Holy Spirit leads them to. If every church had a few people with this gift, there would be much more resources for the kingdom. I am definitely praying for people to receive this gift in our church!

I remember when our church had outgrown our building and had purchased another building, a warehouse, next door. We did not have any money left to carpet the main auditorium. The warehouse had in fact once been a factory, so the floor was not good. One morning I had a telephone call from Mike, our pastor, to say that he had received a very generous cheque from a Vineyard church that would cover the cost of carpeting the whole floor. I cried for about an hour! It really felt as if we were given this gift by God Himself and it touched us deeply that another church would give us so much money, when I am sure they would have found it easy to spend it on their own ministry.

Praise God for this gift!

THE GIFT OF SERVING

This gift is for the servant-hearted. What better example do we have than Jesus? Time after time He showed how to treat others as we would want to be treated. The most humbling occasion was when He washed the dirty feet of the disciples:

> *so he got up from the meal, took off his outer clothing, and wrapped a towel around his waist. After that, he poured water into a basin and began to wash his disciples' feet, drying them with the towel that was wrapped around him.*
>
> **John 13:4–5**

The gift of serving is often a gift that is in the background and is one that may not often get recognized. But the Lord sees it all.

My observation whilst travelling about Britain and abroad, is that in almost every church I visit, a small group of people seem to do most tasks in the church. Not many people volunteer to do the servant-hearted jobs.

I don't think I have ever heard anyone ask for the gift of serving, but we really need it in our churches. Can you imagine what it would be like if a large proportion of a church operated in this gift? It would be amazing!

THE GIFT OF FAITH

I like the definition of this gift in David Pytches' book *Come Holy Spirit*:

> *This gift is a supernatural surge of confidence from the Spirit of God which arises within a person faced with a specific situation or need whereby that person receives a trans-rational certainty and assurance that God is about to act through a word or action. This miracle utterance covers*

creation or destruction, blessing or cursing, removal or alteration.

So God gives the gift of faith when He wants to do something special.

Faith and Finance

I have sometimes been in situations where solutions have seemed impossible. For instance, some time ago, Soul Survivor Watford set out to buy a dilapidated warehouse to use as our church building. At the time there were only fifty people in our congregation and many of them were young non-earners. It was a ridiculous thing to do, since we didn't have enough money for the deposit, let alone the refurbishment costs! But God gave us the gift of faith to believe that He was with us in this and it would all be OK – even though the circumstances said the opposite. I remember it being a very scary time, but we all had an underlying conviction that it would happen and the warehouse would be ours.

Eventually it was!

Once we had purchased it, there was a lot of work to do to make it useable. The refurbishment of the ceiling was an important job that involved replacing all of the existing tiles. We had already done two huge sections of it, but had no money for the third. Sitting on the floor with a few other people, having a rest from sweeping up, I said out loud, "Lord, we know you have all the money that is needed for this ceiling. We ask you to release it now." I knew in my "knower" immediately after praying this prayer that we would get this last area done, even though I was being shouted down by the others there, who were saying that we had no money.

That night, at midnight, I received a telephone call from our pastor, Mike Pilavachi. He was so excited!

"Jeannie, you will never guess what happened tonight at the celebration. Someone handed me a piece of paper and I put it in my pocket. I thought it was their telephone number. I was just getting undressed and looked at the paper. It was a cheque for £1,000!"

It was exactly the amount we needed for the ceiling to be completed. Thank You, Lord!

Many times during that year God gave us the gift of faith to go forward with the refurbishment, and then later to employ people when we didn't know how we would pay them. I remember the first person we employed was our assistant pastor. Fortunately, he didn't realize it, but we only had enough money to pay him his first two months' wages. During his first few weeks of employment we miraculously received cheques through the post from people we did not know, as if the Lord was letting us know that He was with us.

I do not want you to think that we were being irresponsible, employing people when we had no money. We did it because God was giving us the gift of faith. We knew it was of God to do such a thing, and throughout the next few years we repeated it. It was never easy, but God would stir up the gift of faith in us again and again. I would never advocate taking big risks without the gift of faith!

God has blessed us in so many ways in our church, but it is always in the area of finance that we have taken our biggest leaps.

Faith and Miracles

In the New Testament there are many stories where the gift of faith operates simultaneously with another gift, most often the gift of healing. When Jesus called to the man with the withered hand, "Stretch out your hand" (Luke 6:10), He knew by faith that it was about to be healed. Sure enough, "He did so, and his hand was completely restored" (Luke 6:10).

FaILH anD VISION

When God gives people a vision for their group, church or area of responsibility, they need the gift of faith to put the vision into operation.

Many times I have watched Mike Pilavachi come up with the latest vision for Soul Survivor. Each time the task ahead seemed so enormous and so much bigger than the last one we needed faith for. Mike's gift of faith helps him through those first few months of "shouting it out" from the rooftops until everyone has caught the vision. It's only then that, humanly speaking, he sees what an enormous thing the vision is!

At times we can elevate people who have the gift of faith, putting them on a pedestal as if they are superhuman. They are not! We need to remember that they are operating in a gift of the Holy Spirit and in the natural they will have their days of doubt, fear and agonizing, like the rest of us. The difference with them is that their gift carries them through in order to speak faith into others.

We need to honour the Holy Spirit when we see His servants using His gifts. It is all for the glory of Jesus, not the glory of man.

new wine

Many years ago David Pytches launched a new festival called "New Wine". It was a Christian family week of worship, teaching and ministry in the power of the Holy Spirit. At that time in 1989, apart from Spring Harvest, there were only one or two "Bible Weeks" taking place in England. As well as the main meetings, followed by ministry in the power of the Holy Spirit, there was to be an exhibition, a café, a crèche, children's work and youth work. This would obviously mean a lot of organization, plus a lot of money up front to pay out for all the equipment needed. The slight problem here was that there was no money and no administrators with any experience in doing anything like this.

The lack of finance was not going to stop David! God had given him a vision and the gift of faith for this venture. He borrowed £1,000 from nine supportive churches for the necessary deposits for the site and the equipment, with no guarantee that the money could be repaid.

Margaret Maynard, David's former personal assistant, and I began to administrate the conference, despite having had no previous experience of doing anything remotely like it. Everything was done on a shoestring. We started off that first year in Margaret's dining-room with a stapler, a hole-punch, a box of elastic bands and not much else! Our inexperience of using word processors and talking with hire firms showed up on a regular basis. We had no idea how many people would attend the first New Wine Festival, so one day Margaret and I decided that we would go home that night and ask the Holy Spirit to separately tell us, so that when we met up again we would both know the number to aim for. The next day we were pleased to find out that we both had the same number: 1,500 adults. It turned out that this number was exactly the number that eventually booked into the conference for the whole week.

Throughout all this stress and strain David would carry on as if there was nothing at all to worry about. God had given him that gift of faith. We operated by faith in the Lord, but we also had faith in the vision that David was carrying. We caught this vision and saw such an amazing visitation of the Lord during that first conference.

We thank God for His faithfulness to us all those years ago.

THE GIFT OF MERCY

The hallmarks of this gift are compassion, kindness with understanding, leniency and forgiveness.

The mercy gift communicates the essence of Jesus to people in need by way of action. In other words, it reaches out to people who are in need emotionally, physically or spiritually.

To show mercy is to be compassionate in word and deed.

I love this gift. When I first became a Christian I was so broken, and it was the mercy of Jesus expressed sovereignly, but also through other people around me, that ministered to me deeply and opened me up to receive His healing. His compassion and mercy brought relief to me, changing me for ever.

A person with this gift can discern what others are feeling emotionally and will demonstrate compassion and caring to believers and unbelievers alike. The person with this gift wants to bring healing to another's hurt.

Jesus used this gift when healing. The Bible tells us how He was moved by compassion when He encountered disease or death or demonic oppression. It was this gift of mercy that caused Him to act to heal and deliver. He was merciful to the crowds when they had no food in a remote place, producing food in abundance through a miracle. He was merciful to Martha, Mary and their friends just before He raised Lazarus from the dead. He was moved by compassion and mercy when He raised the widow's son from the dead. He showed mercy to the woman about to be stoned to death.

These are just a few examples. There are many more in the gospels for you to read.

It is normal for a person with the gift of mercy to weep the tears of Jesus as they feel His heart for a situation or a person. It is what the psalmist refers to as "deep calling to deep".

I know this is true because it happened to me often during the first year of moving in this gift. I remember once walking into our lounge and seeing some situation of injustice on the TV, and tears began streaming down my face. If I saw a film based on a true story that contained some injustice I would cry for about an hour afterwards. It was very confusing at the time, as I wasn't sure what was happening, but as I learned more about it I became much more comfortable with it.

He has shown you, O mortal, what is good. And what does the Lord require of you? To act justly and to love mercy and to walk humbly with your God.

Micah 6:8

PRAYER

Holy Spirit, thank You for these gifts that You want to release. Jesus, thank You for Your example. Thank You that You ministered in the gifts of the Holy Spirit at all times, and I can too. Thank You that You choose to use me. You know me so well and know which gifts will fit me, and You want to use them through me. Show me which ones you particularly want to teach me about so that I can grow in them to honour and glorify You. Affirm me as I use them so that I know that they are from You. Give me lots of opportunities to use these gifts to build up Your church and to enable unbelievers to know You. Amen.

ACTION

Think about what it would be like to be given a new gift from the Holy Spirit. You may have already used some of the gifts mentioned in this chapter or you may feel you don't operate in them at all. The good news is, you can always ask for more! The Holy Spirit is waiting to be invited to give you new gifts to build up the church and to speak and act into your community.

Which gift or gifts would you like to ask for?

Is there a gift that you are aware you already have that is under-used, and you need God's help to develop?

SCRIPTURES

There are different kinds of gifts, but the same Spirit distributes them. There are different kinds of service, but the same Lord. There are different kinds of working, but in all of them and in everyone it is the same God at work.

Now to each one the manifestation of the Spirit is given for the common good.

1 Corinthians 12:4–7

To one there is given through the Spirit a message of wisdom, to another a message of knowledge by means of the same Spirit, to another faith by the same Spirit, to another gifts of healing by that one Spirit, to another miraculous powers, to another prophecy, to another distinguishing between spirits, to another speaking in different kinds of tongues, and to still another the interpretation of tongues. All these are the work of one and the same Spirit, and he distributes them to each one, just as he determines.

1 Corinthians 12:8–11

Now you are the body of Christ, and each one of you is a part of it. And God has placed in the church first of all apostles, second prophets, third teachers, then miracles, then gifts of healing, of helping, of guidance, and of different kinds of tongues. Are all apostles? Are all prophets? Are all teachers? Do all work miracles? Do all have gifts of healing? Do all speak in tongues? Do all interpret? Now eagerly desire the greater gifts.

1 Corinthians 12:27–31

Follow the way of love and eagerly desire gifts of the Spirit, especially prophecy.

1 Corinthians 14:1

I long to see you so that I may impart to you some spiritual gift to make you strong...

Romans 1:11

Do not neglect your gift, which was given you through prophecy when the body of elders laid their hands on you.

1 Timothy 4:14

....

CHapter 6

THE GIFT OF TONGUES

When the day of Pentecost came, they were all together in one place. Suddenly a sound like the blowing of a violent wind came from heaven and filled the whole house where they were sitting. They saw what seemed to be tongues of fire that separated and came to rest on each of them. All of them were filled with the Holy Spirit and began to speak in other tongues as the Spirit enabled them.

Now there were staying in Jerusalem God-fearing Jews from every nation under heaven. When they heard this sound, a crowd came together in bewilderment, because each one heard their own language being spoken.

Acts 2:1–6

I love this gift. It is audible, it is fascinating.

Can you imagine what it must have been like for the disciples as they waited in the upper room for the gift that had been promised to them by Jesus? The sense of anticipation would have been almost tangible!

In the verses above, we read that the Holy Spirit came *suddenly*, not gradually or quietly, but like a wind that roared like a storm. This was not a gentle, peaceful experience for the disciples: God had come in power by His Holy Spirit and everything was about to change.

The tongues of fire settled on *each one* of them. No one in that room was left out, everyone was filled. They began to speak languages they had never learned, never studied. I wonder what it would have sounded like?

TONGUES ARE FOR EVERYONE TODAY

Sometimes when I have spoken about the gift of tongues at conferences or seminars, people have reacted angrily, telling me that it is not a gift for today, that it was reserved for the early church. There is a school of thought that maintains that tongues died out with the disciples, as it was only given to spread the gospel in the early days of Christianity.

This is not true!

It is as relevant for us today as it was in Acts. It is a fascinating, beautiful and useful gift and can be used in many different ways for many different things. The apostle Paul encouraged the Corinthian church that it was available for all and should not be stifled:

do not forbid speaking in tongues.

1 Corinthians 14:39

It is not obligatory, no one has to do it – it is not binding by law! But Paul does say:

I would like every one of you to speak in tongues...

1 Corinthians 14:5

SO WHAT ARE "TONGUES"?

Speaking in tongues means speaking in an unknown language. It is prayer addressed to Jesus, primarily as a language of love to Him:

For anyone who speaks in a tongue does not speak to people but to God. Indeed, no one understands them; they utter mysteries by the Spirit.

1 Corinthians 14:2

We utter it by the instigation of the Holy Spirit and it is an expression of God's Spirit interacting with our spirit. When we speak out the words of a language we have not learned, we are speaking to Jesus using our spirit, not our mind:

For if I pray in a tongue, my spirit prays, but my mind is unfruitful.

1 Corinthians 14:14

Speaking in tongues builds strength into us:

Anyone who speaks in a tongue edifies themselves...

1 Corinthians 14:4

WHAT DOES IT SOUND LIKE?

When you first speak in tongues it can sometimes sound like baby language with limited words, and it can seem a bit disappointing. Don't be disappointed! It will grow until you have a full release of your own special prayer language. A friend of mine first started speaking in a baby prayer language with just three words when she was vacuuming! Each day that followed she had one or two additional words and eventually she was flowing in her prayer language.

When you first receive the gift you are likely to speak the words very quickly, so it sounds like gobbledegook. If you slow it down, like all language, it has a rhythm and melody to it. It rises and falls. As you continue to use this gift (I suggest you use it for at least ten minutes every day) it begins to sound more expressive and less "flat", similar to any other language spoken across the world.

All language has a melody to it. Think of the Italian language. Say "Spaghetti Bolognese" as an Italian would, and you will hear the music of the language! In the same way, your prayer language has a melody to it, but often we speak it so fast that it sounds like machine-gunfire!

Although we do not understand all of the words we are saying, our minds can sometimes get a sense of what it is, based on the tone or repetition of words or how we feel. It may be that we are confessing something to God using tongues and we have a sense of release. We may be praising God with a tongue and feel joyful or weep tears of love. Or, if we are interceding in prayer using tongues, we may be aware of an urgency or desperation that rises in our hearts. We can stop and start it at will, we are not overtaken by the gift.

Recently, I was at a youth festival and I gave a seminar about the gifts of the Holy Spirit. All the people who wanted to speak in tongues then prayed to receive this gift. Soon, most of them were all happily speaking in their love languages to Jesus. However, one of the girls that I had heard speaking in her new prayer language approached me in tears. She said, "I feel like I am just making it up." I told her that a lot of people think this when they start speaking in their prayer language for the first time. They feel disappointed because they have a preconceived idea about how their prayer language should sound. I encouraged this young lady to start thanking God for what He had given her, to keep using it, and she would soon see it grow and develop.

DIFFERENT KINDS OF TONGUES

In 1 Corinthians Paul speaks of "different kinds of tongues", suggesting that our prayer language can vary depending on what we are doing or how we are feeling. This is definitely my own experience.

For instance, I have used a "deliverance tongue" during prayer ministry. This is not any louder than I would normally speak in tongues, but actually *sounds* like a more authoritative language. It resembles the German language, mixed with something else. It often comes if I encounter someone who has been involved in occult activity, or there is a residing demon. If I pray for them using this particular tongue, their deliverance from the demonic forces oppressing them happens very quickly.

At other times, when I am praying with someone who needs releasing from bondage, I will pray in a particular tongue. Likewise, I speak in a different one when someone is being anointed or released in joy or is receiving healing. I don't plan it this way: it is the Holy Spirit interacting with my spirit, leading me to pray in a specific way.

I am not sure why it happens this way, but I trust the Holy Spirit to lead me. I have talked with other people about this, only to find that they do the same. So be encouraged that God will give you a language special to you, to suit the situation in which you find yourself.

WHEN DO I USE IT?

PRIVATELY

We can use this gift in our private devotional times. It can be used out loud or can be silent, as if we are having a thought. It can be used as praise, intercession or to release emotion. In fact, I have used speaking in tongues to release anger. Years ago I was very upset about a friend who had been trying to conceive for ten years. It was heartbreaking. At the time, I did not know how to process all of my feelings around this. I decided to pray in tongues, allowing the emotions of anger and disappointment to be expressed. Although I did not know specifically the words I was using, as they were not English, I knew that as I was being led by the Holy Spirit I was saying nothing offensive or wrong. After a very short time the anger dispersed and I continued praying for my friend, first of all in tongues and then in English. A couple of months later I learnt that she was pregnant. Praise God!

PUBLICLY

As we saw in Acts chapter 2, tongues can be spoken publicly. On this occasion, a mix of languages was spoken at the same time, so it must have sounded very loud indeed. The disciples were praising God in many different tongues, to the astonishment of the onlookers. A whole crowd composed of nations from around the world came running as they unexpectedly heard their own language in a land foreign to them. As they gathered, the disciples spoke to them about Jesus and many of them were saved.

If we are using this gift during public prayer ministry we will be praying in tongues with our spirit, but with our mind we can be asking Jesus if He wants to say something to the person we are praying for. If they need guidance, we can ask Him for a revelation in the form of a picture, a word of knowledge or a prophecy or, if they are upset, a word of comfort.

The gift of tongues can also be used in a church service during a corporate time of waiting upon the Lord. The model of ministry we use at Soul Survivor is taken from David Pytches' book *Come Holy Spirit* which was based on the ministry of the late John Wimber. David makes the point that when a word is given out publicly in tongues, the interpretation of that tongue should usually be either one of praise to God, or thanksgiving, or a prophetic revelation. Sometimes in a church congregation several people at the same time are receiving a revelation from God. Someone may speak out giving a prophetic word straight after the word in tongues is spoken. This may then be interpreted by the congregation as the "interpretation of the tongue" when in fact it may be a separate prophetic word.

We need to remember that during the public speaking of tongues by the disciples at Pentecost, they were praising God.

We need to follow this example by publicly speaking in tongues in an atmosphere of praise.

HOW to Receive the Gift of tongues

The biggest barrier that prevents people receiving the gift of tongues is that after they have asked for the gift, they fail to make a sound. It takes some courage and can feel a little embarrassing, but it is what is needed to activate this Holy Spirit gift. It is called *speaking* in tongues, so you have to *speak*! At first everyone thinks that they are making up the language themselves, but why would you? When you first learn to swim you have to take your feet off the bottom and launch out, trusting that the water will hold you up. In the same way you need to launch out in this gift, trusting that you will be safe. The Holy Spirit will uphold you. Try not to analyse what is happening with your brain, but receive in faith. Worship Jesus within you, loose your tongue and let go.

There have been times when I have had someone approach me at the end of a seminar and say, "I have asked God for a prayer language but He didn't give it to me." I reply, "Yes He did – you just haven't used it yet!" Remember, God says that we must ask and it will be given to us:

So I say to you: Ask and it will be given to you; seek and you will find; knock and the door will be opened to you. For everyone who asks receives; the one who seeks finds; and to the one who knocks, the door will be opened.

Luke 11:9–10

God does not lie. Go ahead and make a sound in worship to Jesus – loose your tongue, forget yourself, forget your embarrassment and leap out! After you start speaking in tongues, say thank you to the Holy Spirit for giving you this gift and remember that Jesus loves to hear what you are saying because it is worshipping Him.

95

If you do find it difficult to let go, find some friends who speak in tongues to help you. After asking for the gift, ask them to speak out loud in their own prayer language and try to say some of the same sounds as them. As you start to try it, you will be released in your own tongue.

If after trying the above suggestions you still find it difficult to make a sound, just shut your eyes and out loud, pray and choose to bring your intellect or mind to Jesus, and surrender it to Him. You may be trying to analyse things too much.

I have seen children as young as three and four years of age receive the gift of tongues, and the oldest person was over eighty! The young ones in particular have no barriers to receiving, as they are so innocent and unquestioning, and they are often well on their way immediately after asking.

Some Stories

My Mother

One day as I was serving our evening meal, my mother started to tell me about all the people in her church who were better Christians than she was because they prayed in tongues. I replied, "What a load of rubbish – it doesn't mean you are a better Christian if you speak in tongues!" Then I asked her if she wanted to have her own prayer language and receive that gift from the Holy Spirit. She said that she did.

First of all I encouraged her to ask Jesus for this gift and to worship and praise Him. After a minute or two I then said to her, "As I touch your lips, start speaking out." The reason I touched her lips was to encourage her to "go for it" and start making a noise. As soon as I did this, she started to speak in tongues! I continued to dish out the meat and mashed potato onto plates while my Mum began praying in a beautiful language.

After thanking Jesus, I asked my Mum what she thought of all this and she shocked me by saying, "Hmm, it doesn't sound as good as Mrs Brown's prayer language in church." As you can imagine, I told her that she shouldn't under-value this beautiful gift that Jesus had just given her and compare it to anyone else's. Her gift was special to her, given to her by the Holy Spirit who loved her.

SPEAKING ZULU

As I mentioned earlier, a prayer language can start off by sounding like baby language. It seems to grow over a few days before then flowing into a language with different sounds. Once, when I was in South Africa a girl was lying on the floor speaking in tongues in a very unusual way. I asked the Zulu girl next to me if she had any idea what this girl was saying. She started to smile and excitedly said, "She is speaking the Zulu alphabet. That is amazing because she comes from the Congo and doesn't know Zulu!" Apparently, before she began speaking in her prayer language, Jesus was starting her off with this alphabet. Why? I have no idea, but He can do whatever He wants to do!

Another time in South Africa I was praying for a very shy Zulu girl. She really wanted to speak in tongues, so I encouraged her to ask Jesus, as it says in the Bible to "eagerly ask for spiritual gifts". She did so and I did the same thing I had done with my mother. I put my fingers on her lips and asked her to speak out her new language. Amazingly, as she spoke out in her new words, I started speaking the same language simultaneously! We both laughed and decided to start again. Just as before, we both spoke in the same language, and this happened three more times! By this time we were curling up with laughter.

Why did Jesus do that? I don't know, but something I do know is that later on this very shy girl received a public prophetic word from someone during a workshop I was doing, and it really touched her deeply. She had been severely abused when she was a child. The word that had been given caused the suppressed pain of this abuse to come to the surface and

I ended up ministering to her. I think that the time we had together earlier allowed her to trust me later to share her pain with me. What a privilege!

... and Romanian!

I heard a really great story recently. It was at one of the Soul Survivor Festivals and Mike Pilavachi, who was leading the event, had just invited forward any young people who wanted to be filled with the Holy Spirit and receive the gift of tongues. As they flocked forward Mike encouraged those already with this gift to start praising Jesus with him.

At this point a Romanian pastor started to leave the Big Top, irritated by what was happening, as he did not believe in the gift of tongues. Just as he got to the door, over the PA system he heard Mike speaking out in a tongue that he recognized as ancient Romanian.

To the pastor's astonishment, Mike was quoting a couple of lines from an old Romanian poem that had years ago been tattooed on the back of the pastor's father. This poem was very familiar to him from his childhood, as his father had often quoted it to him. It was at that point that the pastor changed his mind about the gift of tongues!

Learning a Lesson

Years ago when I was in Portugal I really wanted to be able to speak the local language, so I went into a shop and decided I would speak out in tongues and see if they would understand what I was saying. Seeing the lady behind the counter, I launched into my prayer language, but she just stared blankly at me. So I smiled at her and left the shop. Afterwards I realized that I had been flippant with the precious God-given gift that was designed to be used in my relationship with Him, to bless Him. I had tried to put Him to the test. I realized this was sinful so I told Him that I was sorry.

The great thing, though, was that Jesus knew I longed to speak to other people in their own language. On two occasions during times of ministry He has given me some words in a language that other people have understood. The first was in Holland when, as a person fell to the ground under the power of the Holy Spirit, I uttered some words in Dutch, and the second was when I spoke Italian to an Italian. It was just four words, but those words gave me so much joy and encouragement!

Keeping the Gift alive

Sometimes people come up to me after I have spoken on the gift of tongues and tell me that they used to have a prayer language, but they do not use it any more because it does nothing for them. My response to that is that this gift is given to them to bless Jesus. I explain that He loves it when we communicate in the freedom of spirit to Spirit, relating to Him in love. Then I encourage them to speak out their language to God, slowing it down and thinking of Jesus as they do so.

It is important that we keep using the gifts we have been given; otherwise they will become stale and our relationship with God will feel more distant and cold.

So keep it alive! Do it often when you are walking, driving the car, at work, and other times throughout the day. You will find you are connecting more and more with Jesus and opening up a channel to hear Him more clearly as you do.

Also, be willing to develop this gift. Ask Jesus for an increase: a worship tongue, a thanksgiving tongue, an intercession tongue or a deliverance tongue. If you keep using it you will discover you have different languages at different times and in different situations.

PRAYER

Thank You, Lord, for this wonderful gift. I want to worship You with sounds that You give me. I bring my mind to You and surrender it. I want to worship You with my spirit and my body. Please give me the gift of tongues. Fill me now with a love language to You. Enable me to use it often and in the ways You show me. I lift my spirit to engage with You, Holy Spirit. Give me this release now in Jesus' name. Amen.

ACTION

Now think of Jesus and how much you love Him. Let your tongue go and make sounds to Him. Speak it out, not worrying what it will sound like. Remember, it may start with just one or two words. Keep practising this and it will grow.

If you would rather meet up with a couple of people who use this gift, then do so. As they lay hands on you, think of how much you love Jesus and get them to speak out in their prayer language. Try and do what they are doing. As you start to make sounds you will start speaking out in your own unique language from the Lord. Enjoy!

SCRIPTURES

... to another speaking in different kinds of tongues...
1 Corinthians 12:10

Anyone who speaks in a tongue edifies themselves...
1 Corinthians 14:4

This is what we speak, not in words taught us by human wisdom but in words taught by the Spirit, explaining spiritual realities with Spirit-taught words.

1 Corinthians 2:13

Therefore, my brothers and sisters, be eager to prophesy, and do not forbid speaking in tongues. But everything should be done in a fitting and orderly way.

1 Corinthians 14:39–40

All of them were filled with the Holy Spirit and began to speak in other tongues as the Spirit enabled them.

Acts 2:4

If I speak in the tongues of men or of angels, but do not have love, I am only a resounding gong or a clanging cymbal.

1 Corinthians 13:1

For they heard them speaking in tongues and praising God.

Acts 10:46

CHAPTER 7

....

THE GIFT OF WORDS OF KNOWLEDGE

Go to the lake and throw out your line. Take the first fish you catch; open its mouth and you will find a four-drachma coin. Take it and give it to them for my tax and yours.

Matthew 17:27

In this passage, Jesus is having a conversation with Peter about the paying of taxes. He tells Peter that in order not to offend the authorities, they must pay taxes as they are due. Instead of digging into his pocket and giving Peter some money, Jesus decides to do something much more creative, illustrating the point clearly by inviting Peter, a fisherman, to go and fish! That way, Peter was likely to remember it for the rest of his life.

Words of knowledge are given to us by God to catch our attention, to help us to remember something important and out of the ordinary. We know the wonderful truth of how God loves us from Scripture, of course, and words of knowledge will never add anything to that, but they are given to remind us that God knows us, knows our circumstances and is with us in them.

A word of knowledge is a specific piece of information that can only be known by supernatural means. In other words, it is given by the Holy Spirit for a particular purpose. It can be about a person's past, present or future, although knowledge about the future is normally referred to as "prophecy", which we will look at in the next chapter.

A word of knowledge can be given and received anywhere at any time, but will most often come during times of prayer ministry when the Holy Spirit is present and wanting to speak, raising faith in the person concerned and releasing encouragement that God *really* knows and understands them.

WHAT WILL THE WORDS OF KNOWLEDGE BE ABOUT?

Anything and everything! The Holy Spirit is not confined to only a few words of knowledge, communicating them to someone every now and again. One of the ways God shows His love to us is to *go beyond* what we can imagine, and when He speaks through someone else about things that no one else knows, or gives a key to unlocking bondage in a life, He wants us to listen.

Words can be about anything from migraines to heart conditions, dreams and visions, to job changes, warnings, encouragements, blessings and challenges. They can be very specific or more general, but they are always, when given in submission to the Holy Spirit, an opportunity for freedom and release.

WATCH AND LEARN

It is important that we do not just launch ourselves into giving words of knowledge without learning how it is done.

Seek out someone you know who uses some of these revelatory gifts and ask them questions. Ask if you can be with them when they minister to others so that you can learn from them. After all, we are all on a lifelong journey of learning.

LOOKING at the LIFE OF JESUS

Jesus, because He spent His life listening closely to what God had to say to Him, frequently moved in words of knowledge. We see Him operating in this gift many times in the gospels. Let's look at two examples of this.

THE Samaritan Woman

When He met the Samaritan woman at the well and told her to go and fetch her husband, she replied that she did not have a husband. Then came the word of knowledge:

Jesus said to her, "You are right when you say you have no husband. The fact is, you have had five husbands, and the man you now have is not your husband. What you have just said is quite true."

John 4:17–18

The woman returned to her village, so amazed that Jesus knew her. The Bible tells us:

Then, leaving her water jar, the woman went back to the town and said to the people, "Come, see a man who told me everything I ever did. Could this be the Messiah?" They came out of the town and made their way toward him.

John 4:28–30

A little later on we read that many Samaritans believed in Jesus because of His encounter with this woman. His word of knowledge to her did not just change her life, but the lives of many people in her village.

ZACCHAEUS

I believe that another time Jesus used a word of knowledge was when He saw Zacchaeus the tax collector peering out of the sycamore tree. He already knew that Zacchaeus cheated people and He completely disarmed him by telling him that He was coming to his house for tea. Jesus knew that because he was a liar and a cheat, Zacchaeus was not used to people coming to his house. He did not have many friends. No one trusted him due to the fact that he made a living from exploitation. Jesus knew the state of his heart and did not judge him or walk away. He loved him into changing. This love changed Zacchaeus so much that he returned the money he had stolen. In fact, he gave back more money than he had originally taken from people.

WORKSHOPS

I like to pass on what I know so that people can benefit from my experience, which includes both the successes and the "failures"! I love to lead seminars or workshops on the gifts of the Holy Spirit, giving plenty of space to practise them. Sometimes, when teaching about words of knowledge, I have asked people to wait on God, asking Him to show them specific health problems, primarily in those who are present in the room. Information from the Holy Spirit will then begin to come to their minds, often in pictures. Sometimes actual words will pass before their eyes. Another time they may feel heat or cold in some part of their body or perhaps a sudden pain or ache in places that are normally pain free. Sometimes the pictures seem unusual or amusing, but quite often the words given out which sound the most outlandish are the ones that people respond to, saying that they have that particular condition.

When the Holy Spirit is honoured and welcomed and given room to speak, He will do just that. Learning to operate in words of knowledge is not difficult and is not just for the few.

WORDS OF KNOWLEDGE AND PHYSICAL HEALING

Years ago in St Andrew's Church we used to offer prayer ministry after the Sunday services for people who needed healing. We would pray and ask God for words of knowledge for medical conditions, knowing that God wanted to heal people.

Just to encourage you, I want to tell you that God will use anyone who is willing to accept this gift, even if it doesn't always go the way you think it will! I have very clear memories of some embarrassing situations in the early days of these prayer times when I spoke out what I believed were words of knowledge.

I remember calling out a word that I had seen when I shut my eyes. There was no way I knew how to pronounce what I could see, but many years previously I had told Jesus that I was willing to be a fool for Him, so I launched out and said: "There is someone here with a problem with their oso-fee-gus."

Everyone there burst out laughing! I had no idea what I had said that was so funny and waited to see if anyone would respond. At the end of the prayer time, a man came to the microphone and said: "I would like to thank the young lady who spoke out about my condition. I did have a problem with my oesophagus, but Jesus has just healed it."

Everyone laughed and clapped and I realized that my pronunciation had been wrong, but Jesus had still healed the condition. The great thing about using the gifts of the Holy Spirit is that you also get educated in the process!

My next embarrassing experience happened when, in another church service, I called out: "There is someone here with a problem with their prostate gland. I think it's a man."

Once again the whole church burst out with uncontrollable laughter. I thought I had messed up the pronunciation again, but once again at the end of the service a man made his way to the microphone and said: "I believe that Jesus has just healed my prostate gland and I would like to inform the young lady that – yes – I am a man!"

I laughed along with everyone else without really

understanding what I was laughing at. Later on my vicar came up to me and told me that only men have a prostate gland. Brilliant! Another opportunity to learn about naming parts of the body I did not previously know existed.

These were my most embarrassing moments. I have had others but they are probably not as funny. The point is, we will all make mistakes when we use spiritual gifts because we are human. We just need to speak out what we think we are seeing and remain open for Jesus to tell us more. We can ask Him questions whenever we need an answer so that we increase in our knowledge of the use of this gift.

more amazing stories

for the first time

During a recent seminar some young people were asking the Holy Spirit for words of knowledge about conditions in the people present that Jesus wanted us to pray for.

One young girl, who had never received words of this sort before, was suddenly given the names of four different medical conditions. I asked her how she had received these words. She said that in her hand she could feel the weight of four different organs of the body that she had named. She could also see them.

Following prayers for people in the room, this girl came up for prayer herself in response to another word of knowledge. As others laid hands on her she testified to the fact that Jesus had healed her of Irritable Bowel Syndrome, which caused acute anxiety, cramps and bloating in her stomach. This young girl had never given or received any words of knowledge before this time. She was amazed that Jesus had done so much in and through her in the space of about fifteen minutes!

AN AUSTRALIAN ADVENTURE

In Australia a few years ago I remember leading a workshop on prophecy. As we were in a circle waiting on the Holy Spirit for revelation, an older man pointed to a middle-aged woman and asked her if she had Aboriginal heritage. I remember being bewildered by this, as the woman was blonde and fair skinned, with not a trace of the distinctive Aborigine features. She looked surprised and told the man that she didn't. He looked very embarrassed and went red in the face, clearly wishing that the floor would open up and swallow him! At that moment I called out to him, asking him to tell me what had come into his head as we waited on God. He told me he had seen a picture of an Aborigine, and when I asked him what had popped into his head about the Aborigine people when he had received the picture, he told me: "That they are a people who have had something taken from them that is rightfully theirs."

As he said these words the woman burst into tears and some people went to pray with her. Later she explained that when the man had spoken these words, it was as if something had risen up inside her and she felt released.

So a word of knowledge can be accurate even if at first it seems unlikely. If God has spoken about something, it is important we do not discount it just because it is not obvious at first.

HEALING FROM GRIEF

Once, when a man came forward and asked for prayer, some words came into my head. I could hear the words "I wasn't there, I wasn't there, I wasn't there" being spoken by the man's voice, but he was standing in front of me praying silently. I knew God was speaking and I believe it is important never to add anything to what He is saying, so we need to just say it in the way that we have received it.

I spoke out these three words three times to the man I was praying for. He burst into tears and sobbed for a while.

When he had recovered enough to speak, he said that a few years previously his mother had died in hospital. He had been a thousand miles away in another country and he "wasn't there". He had never said goodbye to her and had grieved deeply about that. I told him it was never too late, that he could say it there and then. He could tell Jesus what he never said to his mother and Jesus would pass it on. The man did just that, and after he had finished he said that he now had space inside where the grief had been. Isn't that wonderful?

That is what our Jesus the Healer is like. Sometimes these words arrive in our heads very softly and we can so easily miss them or ignore them. I am so glad I didn't ignore those words. It can be easier not to speak out what Jesus gives us. We worry so much that we may get it wrong. Let us decide to speak out and risk making a mistake. We can always say sorry if we think that, on reflection, what we said was more us than God. After all, what is the worst thing that can happen?

How Do I Receive a Word of Knowledge?

Words of knowledge can come when we are in an attitude of prayer, worship and openness, as some specific language or as a picture or as a series of pictures. They can also come as physical manifestations in our own bodies. If we are practising in a group using words of knowledge, then we can ask the Holy Spirit to show us physical conditions, ailments or diseases that people may have in the room. As I have previously said, our bodies can respond with sensations of heat or cold or we may have a sudden or growing pain in a part of our body that is usually pain free. This is the Holy Spirit communicating something specific to us for someone in the room, and it will not last a long time.

AM I MAKING IT UP?

Sometimes we can worry that we are making all this up. But why would we? If our motivation is to see the body of Christ healed and we have surrendered our imagination to Jesus, why would God not give us words that would enable His people to walk in freedom?

In order to lead people away from the worry that they are making it up, I usually ask them to surrender their imagination to Jesus. He made it, so it is safe with Him. Then I encourage them to specifically ask the Holy Spirit for words of knowledge for people in the room with medical conditions or who need emotional healing.

JUST GO WITH IT

I remember that during one of these times, someone gave out a word about a very unusual medical condition which I had not heard of before. They followed the word with, "I also see a bowl of peas." Everyone laughed, as it seemed so totally unconnected to any medical condition. Later on someone came forward to say that he was responding to the word about the medical condition and that the bowl of peas also referred to him, since he "peed a lot"! This started people laughing again, including the man who had come forward. He then added, "It's not usually green, though!" I love it when Jesus takes away all the intensity of a situation through humour.

WHAT IF I GET IT WRONG?

If you realize that fear of making a mistake holds you back from receiving or giving words of knowledge, here is a prayer you can use:

Jesus, I am sorry that I have allowed the fear of making a mistake to get in the way of receiving or giving out words of knowledge. I choose to bring that fear to You and surrender it. I know that Your perfect love casts out fear. Fill me with Your Holy Spirit so that I will boldly step out when You give me the opportunity. Thank You, Lord. Amen.

We need to realize that the enemy does not want us to move in the gifts of the Holy Spirit. He doesn't want us to get equipped and grow in these gifts. He doesn't want people to get healed and he will do everything he can to stop it, which includes trying to intimidate us, and making us anxious about making mistakes. We need to always remember that God is so much more powerful than Satan! We need to get inferior thoughts out of our heads and just get on with it.

When we are learning and practising in a group, we should agree together from the outset that it is acceptable to make a mistake. If we do this, then no one is going to blame us if occasionally we get it wrong. After all, we all make mistakes when we are learning. How many times did we fall off our bike before we learned how to ride it properly?

The good news is that sometimes you will be getting it gloriously right!

PRAYER

Thank You, Jesus, for this wonderful gift. I would love to see You using this gift through me to bring people closer to You. Please enable me to communicate in this supernatural way. I offer up my imagination for You to use. Please give me revelation in words and pictures for people and situations that I have no natural means of knowing. Give me many opportunities to step out using this gift. Give me courage and boldness to push through my feelings of embarrassment and fear. Use me to bring Your love and insight into a hurting world. Give me wisdom to know how to be sensitive in how and when to use this gift. Please encourage me and fill me with this gift now. Amen.

ACTION

Have the stories I have told inspired and encouraged you? When God speaks about a life, He is speaking from the place of knowing it intimately. God does not guess and He will never make mistakes. He trusts us to communicate His heart to people through words of *His* perfect knowledge of someone's life – their past experiences or present situation. He understands how just one word or picture or physical manifestation in the Holy Spirit can turn a life around. People respond to God when He tells them He knows them.

How would you like God to use you in this gift?

Have you had a word of knowledge from God through someone that has set you free? Take some time to thank God for that word now.

SCRIPTURES

The man of God sent word to the king of Israel: "Beware of passing that place, because the Arameans are going down there." So the king of Israel checked on the place indicated by the man of God. Time and again Elisha warned the king, so that he was on his guard in such places.

2 Kings 6:9–10

So they inquired further of the Lord, "Has the man come here yet?"

And the Lord said, "Yes, he has hidden himself among the supplies."

1 Samuel 10:22

Now while he was in Jerusalem at the Passover Festival, many people saw the signs he was performing and believed in his name. But Jesus would not entrust himself to them, for he knew all people. He did not need any testimony about mankind, for he knew what was in each person.

John 2:23–25

When Jesus saw that a crowd was running to the scene, he rebuked the impure spirit. "You deaf and mute spirit," he said, "I command you, come out of him and never enter him again."

Mark 9:25

THE GIFT OF PROPHECY

In this chapter I will explain what the gift of prophecy is and how it operates. The following chapter, "Practising Prophecy", is a practical guide to stepping out in this wonderful gift.

WHAT IS PROPHECY?

Prophecy can be described as being given knowledge of the future by God. Mike Bickle from Kansas City has described it in three stages. First there is *supernatural revelation*, second comes *interpretation* and third is the *application*.

In other words, we see or hear what God wants to say, we explain the significance of what is being revealed and then we apply what has been revealed into a situation or circumstance.

When God wants to speak to a group of believers or an individual, He will almost always use His prophets to act as His mouthpiece. The prophets will then communicate whatever God wants to say, however He wants to say it. Messages are given as warnings, as encouragements, for comfort, for instruction and for the strengthening and building up of the church.

The Bible tells us that the gift of prophecy is something to treasure:

Follow the way of love and eagerly desire gifts of the Spirit, especially prophecy.

1 Corinthians 14:1

HOW IS PROPHECY COMMUNICATED?

God is never boring and He will choose many different ways of speaking to His people. He speaks through riddles, dreams, drama, nature, song, poetry, art, dance, visions, preaching and teaching, to name a few! Let's look at a few examples:

RIDDLES

CRUMBS

Recently I was praying with a young woman and I saw two pictures. I said to her, "I think you may have asked God for a sandwich, but you feel that He has only given you crumbs."

This first part was really a word of knowledge, but I could sense that God wanted to speak into some disappointment in her life that was acting as a barrier to the new things Jesus wanted to give her. As the woman cried, I asked her to give her disappointment to Jesus, and as she did, I spoke out a prophetic word, saying, "I sense God is saying that many crumbs make up a sandwich!"

I then received an interpretation from God and went on to tell her that Jesus was going to continue to answer her prayers bit by bit, until she had fully received what He wanted to give her and what she had asked for.

What began as a riddle became a life-changing event.

UMBRELLAS

"Don't go out in the rain wearing a rain hat when you can take an umbrella!" This was a prophetic word I received while in a meeting, so I shared it and asked the Holy Spirit for the interpretation. I sensed that what He was saying was that we should not just look after our own needs, but go out expecting to make provision for others too. After the service, two people approached me to tell me that this was a significant prophecy for them at that time.

As you can imagine, this was a great encouragement to me. To be honest, I had felt a little foolish speaking these words in public, but as I did not want to grieve the Holy Spirit, I decided to take the leap.

DRAMA

Sometimes God speaks through drama. During a meeting at a John Wimber conference I attended, I noticed some men and women miming prophetic words in different places around the auditorium. I felt a little uneasy about it as it looked a little bizarre at first, but eventually I could see what they were doing. A man in the gallery looked like he was washing windows. A woman in the stalls looked like she was sweeping the aisles. Others were acting similar things. John let it continue for some minutes, prayed and called the people forward. He asked them what they were miming and they explained they were cleaning and clearing out bags of rubbish. John was quiet for a moment and then said, "The Lord is cleaning up His church!" At that point, the Holy Spirit fell on the congregation and we had an amazing night!

There are many other ways God speaks prophetically and I will include some stories in this chapter as we continue, but at this point let me remind you to honour those who function freely in the prophetic, as they are a gift of God to His church. They may not always act or speak in ways we understand or find easy, but God knows how He wants to communicate, so we need to stay open to Him.

JESUS AND PROPHECY

In the Old Testament there are over forty prophecies foretelling the life and death of Jesus. These prophecies were spoken without the prophet knowing when they would be fulfilled. They probably faced ridicule from people who did not understand them, but they were willing to be fools for God's sake, speaking out His words about the future. Sometimes, prophecies about Jesus were given in the middle of a psalm, either about His character or what was going to happen to Him on the cross.

Jesus often prophesied His own death and resurrection as well as things that were happening around Him. One of Jesus' best-known prophecies was addressed to Peter:

"Truly I tell you," Jesus answered, "today – yes, tonight – before the rooster crows twice you yourself will disown me three times."

Mark 14:30

Before He said this, Jesus had just prophesied:

You will all fall away...

Mark 14:27

He went on to quote a prophecy from the Old Testament about how the shepherd would be struck and how the sheep would be scattered.

Have a good look in the gospels and see how many times Jesus prophesied. It is a lot easier, by the way, if you look in the versions that have the words of Jesus printed in red!

A PROMISE FROM tHE BIBLE

In the last days, God says, I will pour out my Spirit on all people. Your sons and daughters will prophesy, your young men will see visions, your old men will dream dreams. Even on my servants, both men and women, I will pour out my Spirit in those days, and they will prophesy.

Acts 2:17–18

These words in Acts were originally spoken by the prophet Joel in the Old Testament before the birth of Jesus. At Pentecost, when the Holy Spirit descended in power, He released the disciples in spiritual gifts, as Jesus had promised. The reminder of the promise from Joel was an encouragement to them, as it should be to us today. The gifts of the Holy Spirit are available to us at all times, as He has promised. The promise that men and women will prophesy shows that God loves to give prophecy as a gift.

We can all prophesy, but we have not all been anointed specifically with the gift of prophecy. Everyone is different and the Holy Spirit gives different gifts for the building up of His church.

GIVING a PROPHETIC WORD IS JUST LIKE DOING a BUNGEE JUMP!

If you have the gift of prophecy, it is important that you know how to deliver God's words to people with wisdom and love. Even if it is a tough word, it will still carry the grace of God.

Giving a word of prophecy can feel, at times, like taking a bungee jump into the unknown. I recently saw a film of my son-in-law doing a bungee jump in South Africa. He was jumping off the highest bridge in the southern hemisphere and the look on his face before he jumped was priceless! It was a mixture of raw fear and total disbelief that he was in that place, about to jump. Suddenly, after winking at the camera, he was off into the deep ravine, trusting in the rope to hold him and keep him safe.

When giving a prophetic word, by whatever means, you hope that God will be your rope, holding on to you to save you from a disastrous end! In fact, He does just that. Giving a prophetic word is exhilarating, even though at times it can feel terrifying, so that you will want to repeat the experience again and again.

YOU WON'T ALWAYS GET IT RIGHT

I have some good news for you: you will make mistakes sometimes! I am comforted by the truth that I do not have to be perfect and if I give a prophetic word that is not 100 per cent correct, I can trust God to cover it. As long as my motive is to bless and my heart is to show the love of God to people, I will keep having a go. Also keep in mind that if you don't speak out a word the Holy Spirit is giving you, then you are denying the other person a blessing. Of course, the Holy Spirit can give the word to someone else instead, but then you will be the one who misses out on the blessing of being used by God.

> But the one who prophesies speaks to people for their strengthening, encouraging and comfort.
>
> **1 Corinthians 14:3**

We must be careful to keep this verse in our minds when prophesying to people. If someone tells you are going to lose all your friends, that your house will burn down and that you will contract a life-threatening disease, that doesn't fit in with Scripture, does it? It certainly doesn't fit in with the specific scripture above. You may get asked to leave the church or be called a false prophet! On the other hand, if you have given words that have brought life and hope to a person, that would be a cause of great excitement and encouragement.

We need to make sure that when we give a word from God, it complies with that verse of Scripture. Do a quick check before speaking it out and ask yourself, "Is this prophecy strengthening, encouraging and comforting?"

AGABUS

To show you that prophets are not always expected to be infallible, let me introduce you to a prophet called Agabus from the book of Acts. Agabus correctly prophesied that a famine was coming and, as these verses show, the disciples responded to the word in practical ways:

> *One of them, named Agabus, stood up and through the Spirit predicted that a severe famine would spread over the entire Roman world. (This happened during the reign of Claudius.) The disciples, as each one was able, decided to provide help for the brothers and sisters living in Judea. This they did, sending their gift to the elders by Barnabas and Saul.*
>
> **Acts 11:28–30**

However, it seemed that Agabus did not get it completely right. We see later in Acts 21 that he saw in the Spirit how Paul would be bound and imprisoned, and then he mistakenly assumed that it would be the Jews who bound him, when it was in fact the Gentiles. It was a Roman soldier (a Gentile) who, in the end, physically bound Paul, as it was his duty as a soldier to arrest anyone who was a trouble-maker. Agabus and the elders of the church begged him not to go to Jerusalem, but Paul knew he had to go because God had shown him already what was going to happen (Acts 21:13)

I find this story of Agabus encouraging, because we can all worry that we may not have got a prophecy exactly right. Some of us worry so much that we fail to speak it out.

Sometimes when we are starting off using this gift it may well be more like "blessed thoughts" than prophecy. But this isn't going to harm anyone, is it? As we start out, as long as we are honest and not making something up that is not true, then we will soon learn how to listen to the words from the Holy Spirit.

> *For we know in part and we prophecy in part... For now we see only a reflection as in a mirror...*
>
> **1 Corinthians 13:9–12**

WORDS OF WARNING AND DIRECTION

Words of prophecy can sometimes be given as a warning or to provide direction in our lives, but we need to handle it very carefully if we believe we have one of these words. Imagine if you told someone they were going to have a car accident and then they did. You could think that because the person *did* have an accident during that day, it validates your prophetic word. In reality, it could be that you suggested something to their unconscious mind and that they went through the rest of the day expecting something bad to happen. At this point, fear could have entered into them and they could have convinced themselves that they were going to have an accident. As Job put it:

> *What I feared has come upon me; what I dreaded has happened to me.*

Job 3:25

It could be that the person then, due to anxiety, does not drive as competently as they normally would, and the "prophecy" comes true! We need to realize how powerful words can be and we need to remember that our words must strengthen, encourage and comfort.

Continuing the illustration, if you did have a word that seemed to indicate a tragedy such as a car crash, you could frame it sensitively to the person, saying something like, "I have a strong sense of God's love for you. He wants you to be very careful and prayerful about your driving." At that point we can also pray for them and ask God for His protection.

I have heard of people being told the most outrageous things. Most recently someone was told that they would give birth to a disabled child. How was that word helpful? Fear entered the person and then they could think of nothing else! The person given the so-called prophecy wasn't even pregnant or planning to be in the near future. But you can be sure that from that moment she wasn't relishing the thought of any future pregnancy or birth.

MY FRIEND LUCY

I remember one occasion when I needed to be extremely careful when giving a prophetic word. I had a word for my friend, Lucy, who was pregnant at the time. I didn't want to frighten her, but I really felt that she shouldn't go and have her child at the local hospital. It would have been wrong to have told her not to use this hospital for the birth because I felt that something bad would happen. So instead I telephoned her and asked her if she realized that she could in fact have her baby at any hospital. Her mother lived a four-hour drive away, so I asked her if she had considered giving birth at a hospital near to her mother. Then I explained that our daughter had done this and had gone just over two weeks before her due date to stay near a hospital of her choosing.

I encouraged Lucy that she would have her mother close by and she could go there for a week after the birth. Lucy seemed relieved when I said all this to her. She then admitted that for some reason she didn't feel very confident about going to her local hospital. She said that as I suggested going to another hospital she felt a sense of relief and knew that it was the right thing to do. That day Lucy made enquiries as to her options. She did go and stay with her mother and gave birth to a lovely baby boy at the local hospital. Because the hospital was not in a big town it was not very busy and Lucy ended up receiving five-star treatment! At the time of Lucy's delivery there was a report in our local paper about the lack of care in the local maternity unit of the hospital. It said that the shortage of staff was putting mothers' and babies' lives at risk.

In the above scenario, I didn't have a dream, a word or a picture. I just had a "knowing" that this would not be the best option for my friend. I waited for a while, praying about it to know what to do with this "knowing". The burden increased to such an extent that I knew I would have to say something. After asking the Lord how to approach the subject, I realized that the best way would be what I did in telephoning her. This gave Lucy a way out – she could have very easily said no to my suggestion. It is always a good idea to offer anything you sense you have been given, rather than state it as a certainty. The person receiving the prophecy needs to have a sense in their spirit that the word given is from the Lord before acting on it.

BE CAREFUL WHAT YOU SAY

We need to be very careful when praying for people who are sick that we do not prophesy what we are *hoping* will happen. It is very difficult to be impartial if it is someone we care deeply about. These people are likely to be very vulnerable and desperate to hear from God that they are going to recover their health.

I heard of a couple who were expecting a child after many miscarriages. They were given a prophecy that they would have a child that would be perfectly healthy. The child was born with brain damage. Can you imagine what that did to the family's faith? We need to be aware that we are human and our desire is that all will be well, but sometimes life does not work out that way. We need to hold back on this type of prophecy and leave it to those who are more experienced on this journey.

Likewise, it is good to avoid adding the "This is what God says..." prefix to any prophetic word you are giving. It is better to say something like, "I feel that God is saying" or "I sense in my spirit that..." That way, the person does not feel manipulated or controlled and retains their ability to choose whether to act on the word or not.

If you have a word that is a warning, then it would be good to share it with a leader of your church or someone in authority before declaring it publicly, and remember that God will never confirm a word that is contrary to Scripture.

we can all PROPHesy

We may not have all been anointed with the gift of prophecy, but the Bible tells us we can *all* prophesy.

When I have given seminars on the gifts of the Holy Spirit, at the end I have often encouraged a time of asking the Holy Spirit for prophetic words. Most of the people, young or old, who ask God for a prophetic word have never given out even a private word before, let alone one in a large gathering of people. At the beginning I usually get everyone to raise their hand if they agree that it is acceptable that anyone can make a mistake. We agree together that we can practise and risk getting it wrong. I really believe that our Father in heaven looks down on us and is pleased that we are willing to be used by Him and prepared to look foolish. We usually have so many words given that we have to stop, so that we have time to pray for those who respond! We have often had more than forty people responding at a time. Some of the words cause people to weep as they are touched by the Holy Spirit in a significant way. I usually go along the line of people with a microphone so that the people who prophesied can be encouraged by the person who received the word.

Last year, after one such seminar, a young person came up to me and nervously told me that during the time of prophesying he had "seen" a large eagle flying around the room. He looked very affected and shaken by what he had seen, but had no idea what it might mean. Suddenly, I remembered that in Deuteronomy 32:11 there is a passage that speaks of the eagle flying under the nest, ready to catch the baby eagles on the pinions of his wings as they learn to fly. Excitedly I explained this, and we both laughed as we realized that all those speaking out in prophecy were just like those baby birds, learning to fly in the Spirit, with their Daddy ready to catch them when they got it wrong. God's presence with us was an encouragement to us all to go for it!

Submitted to the Leadership

It is important to remember that at whatever level of prophecy we operate, we are all under the authority of the pastor of the church, or the leader of our youth group or ministry team. Sometimes people may attempt to abuse their gift as a means of controlling others or gaining notoriety. If this is the case, a wise leader may ask us to cease prophesying for our own protection, as well as for those we minister to. We do not want loose cannons in our churches! It can be frustrating for pastors of the church when one of the congregation is unwilling to come under authority.

Have confidence in your leaders and submit to their authority, because they keep watch over you as those who must give an account. Do this so that their work will be a joy, not a burden, for that would be of no benefit to you.
Hebrews 13:17

Receiving a Prophetic Word

When we are given a prophetic word it can be a lifeline for us – something we hold on to while we are waiting for a breakthrough. This happened to me a few years ago.

There came a time when our church had outgrown the warehouse in which we met. Out of the blue, an estate agent rang the church office to say that the building next door was for sale. Would we be interested? We were, but we had no money. The people who owned the building were in no hurry to move out, however, so we had to be patient and play a waiting game without knowing how we would eventually pay for it.

Soon after this I was in Holland at the Soul Survivor Festival and one day went into the team room for a coffee. I greeted a man who was sitting there drinking his coffee.

He said to me, "Oh hello, who are you? I can see the Holy

Spirit on you. What are you doing here?"

I told him my name and explained that I had just been speaking about the Holy Spirit in a seminar. I then asked him what he was doing there.

He told me, "I have been leading a seminar – *you will get the building* – and now I am going to clean the toilets!"

Astounded, I asked him to repeat this. Five more times he said, "You will get the building."

Still stunned, I proceeded to tell him that we had no money. He told me to trust the Lord for it. This is the first and only time I have heard of a prophetic word in mid-sentence!

Throughout the buying of the building, which lasted about a year, I held on to this prophecy and when anyone doubted we would get the building, I would remind them of it.

CHECK IT OUT

It is important that when we receive a prophecy of any kind, we weigh it against Scripture. No prophecy that is from God will contradict the Bible. We can also ask the Holy Spirit to confirm it in different ways, particularly if the word is a directional one. In this case, ask God for a confirming word or two from other sources.

PROPHECY BRINGS HOPE

Each time we receive words from God we will be encouraged.

Prophetic words can be healing words. Once I attended a leaders' conference after nursing my husband Ken for a long period through a life-threatening illness that meant that he could hardly walk. During the conference, attendees could sign up for a session of individual prophecy. As I was feeling spiritually and emotionally drained, I signed up for a session.

I walked into the room and saw four people in the centre

of a circle of chairs. Two other people were sitting around the room. I chose a chair with plenty of empty chairs either side of it. This gave me a great sense of privacy. I had been instructed to sit down and shut my eyes and just wait. After a while someone approached me and whispered in my ear that they saw me sitting at a craft table with bits of coloured paper, tearing them up, and the things I had created were beautiful. Hearing this, I burst into tears. This first word was in fact a word of knowledge. During the previous five months I had to be in the house a lot looking after Ken, and to get away from the mundane, everyday work I would go up into my craft room and make greeting cards to sell to a local shop. This was the place where I could stop thinking and immerse myself in something that I enjoyed. I cried even more as I realized that through this word Jesus was telling me that He saw me. He knew about my sense of loneliness during this time and I hadn't been forgotten.

After a while someone else approached me and whispered in my ear a prophetic word that consisted only of two words: "He understands." On hearing this, my tears changed to loud sobs. Such simple words, but they meant such a lot to me. Inside I had felt numb with tiredness, unable to pray, stressed and weary, but He understood. He knew why I kept myself distant from Him. He understood the things that I couldn't understand. After a while someone came over and suggested that I seek prayer ministry during the evening meeting. I left the room soon after, but continued to cry for the next hour!

Jesus was at work in me. During the evening session I went forward for prayer. Jesus showed me that I had been holding on to my husband. I realized that I needed to give up the role of being a nurse and become a wife again. Because my husband had been ill for so long I had forgotten how to relate to him other than as "my patient". I wanted my husband back: I missed him! It was time to surrender "my patient" to Jesus in exchange for my husband who belonged to Jesus. As I did this, I was filled with such love, joy and hope for the future. Thank you, Jesus.

PRƏYER

Jesus, thank You that You fully know me. I want to
hear and recognize Your voice speaking to me. Open
my ears to hear words of comfort, strength and
encouragement. I eagerly desire this gift so that I can
bring Your revelation to others. Speak to me in ways
that I will understand. I offer up my imagination to
You because You made it and can use it to show me
dreams and visions. Speak to me, Lord, when I sleep.
Give me wisdom to know when and how to use this
gift. Amen.

ACtION

The Bible says, "For we know in part and we prophesy in
part..." (1 Corinthians 13:9), so we know that we will never see
everything that God sees. Instead, the Holy Spirit has chosen
to give us glimpses of how God sees us and His world through
the gift of prophecy, and it is wonderful! We should all desire to
prophesy, and we should remember to be thankful for those who
are anointed more fully to speak from the heart of God, to us and
our world.

Do you long to prophesy more?

When was the last time you asked God to give you a word of
prophecy? You can always ask Him now! Just say to Him, "Do You
want to say something, Lord?" Remember to ask Him this when
you are with a group of people too.

CHAPTER 9

....

PRACTISING PROPHECY

Open wide your mouth and I will fill it.

Psalm 81:10

It is all very well learning about the gift of prophecy, but unless we launch out and practise it, all we will have is head knowledge. In this chapter I will offer some practical help, encouraging you to become familiar with the prophetic in a safe environment.

Obviously these are only my ideas and I am not suggesting for a minute that I am teaching you everything on this subject. I want to encourage you to read other books about it, chat to people who prophesy often and even start up your own "prophetic jam" at church or university.

So here we go.

PREPARING TO HEAR MORE

If you are going travelling, you take time to prepare your route, packing your backpack or suitcase with everything you need for the journey. It's the same with the journey into the prophetic. We need to be ready when God wants to speak. Below are some suggestions I hope you will find helpful.

KEEP ASKING

We have seen in a previous chapter that when we ask Him, God generously gives us what we ask for, because He is a good Father. Don't forget to keep asking Him for words of prophecy. Sometimes we expect to be able to prophesy, but we have not taken time to pray about receiving the gift from the Holy Spirit in humility and thankfulness. It is not a free-for-all. The gift is given within a relationship of love. So ask away!

THE NIGHT-TIME ROUTINE

Be prepared for God to speak to you in the night. Scripture has many stories of this happening to people. Remember Samuel? Keep a pen and paper by your bed so that you will be ready for any prophetic dreams or words that the Holy Spirit may give you in the night or early morning. It is also handy to have ready a small torch.

DO YOU WANT TO SPEAK, LORD?

When you are praying for someone, always remember to ask God if He has anything to say. We can sometimes get so caught up in our own prayers that we forget that God may be trying to get a word in! Give the Holy Spirit space to speak specific things if He wants to.

YOU'RE NOT ALONE

Get together with a small group of friends who are also hungry to practise prophecy. It should not be a "heavy" time, but a time when you can learn from God and one another in safety, taking risks without worrying about the consequences too much.

Eyes and Ears

Consciously activate your spiritual "hearing and seeing". This does not mean you will live your life in a holy bubble, but it does mean that you are able to remain on God's wavelength, ready to see or hear what He is showing you.

MODELS FOR PRACTISING HEARING GOD IN A GROUP

When you are ready to meet with or lead a group of people to hear from God, it may help you to have some ideas as to how to go about it. I have given you some models for this here, which have been tried and tested many times with great success, so choose one and give it a go. Remember, you don't need to be perfect and making mistakes is part of learning.

The Hot Seat

Form a circle of four to six people with someone in the middle sitting in the "hot seat". Then lay hands on the seated person, asking the Holy Spirit to bring prophetic words. Listen carefully and prayerfully and be open to receive anything He gives you.

Face to Face

Choose a few willing people to stand at the front facing the rest of the group. Ask for prophetic words. Get people to put up their hands when they get a word or a picture for any one of those at the front.

Hands Up!

Ask the group to form lines, all facing the front, and pray for prophetic words to come by the Holy Spirit. Invite people to put up their hand before they speak if they receive words or pictures.

Ask people to respond to the words given at the end of the session, calling them out to the front. Go along this line, asking which one of the words was significant for them, making sure that people can opt out if they do not want to share. At this point, ask others to come and pray for them.

THE CLOTHES I CHOSE

Sometimes the Holy Spirit speaks by using the clothes we are wearing to illustrate a word: perhaps a slogan on a T-shirt or a piece of jewellery. Form a circle and ask people to look at each other, asking the Lord if He wants to speak in this way. Pick a starting-point and hear from everyone who has something from God.

PICK A PERSON

Every week choose the names of one or two people from your small group that you will pray for during the week, asking the Holy Spirit for words for them. When you receive something, write it down and give the words out publicly (if appropriate) when you next meet. If the person begins to cry as the Holy Spirit ministers to them through the word, just lay hands on them and pray for them. We found this to be a great way of hearing God for each other in our Staff Team.

When you lay hands on someone it should be done gently. The purpose of it is to engage with the Holy Spirit for that person in a clearer way than if you were over the other side of the room. As you do it, remain open and expectant of the Lord, and if after a few minutes you have a picture or a word for the person, ask the Lord what it means. When you feel you have an answer, tell the person.

HOW DOES GOD SPEAK?

God likes variety! He does not confine Himself to speaking in just one or two ways. We can expect a prophetic word to be communicated in a whole variety of ways and in all sorts of environments. Here are just a few so you know what to expect as you develop in this gift:

- God speaks in pictures and images. They can be moving or still, complex or simple, full of colour or plain.
- There can be just one word that God gives you which, when you speak it out, activates a whole sentence or phrase.
- God can put thoughts into your head and a "knowing" of what it all means. These thoughts are similar to your normal thoughts, but you will find they don't drift away but stay in your head, getting louder until you speak them out.
- You may see a sentence passing before your eyes.
- You may suddenly speak out some words that you had not thought about previously.
- God may remind you of something you have seen or done the previous day and speak something fresh through it today.
- You may have a dream, with or without verses of Scripture.
- God may draw your attention to an object in the room, or, as I have said previously, an item of clothing the person is wearing.

Here are some examples of how God has spoken in the ways outlined above:

A RED T-SHIRT

Some time ago, Mike Pilavachi was speaking at a seminar and was asking God for prophetic words. As he did this, I suddenly noticed a girl wearing a red T-shirt and heard the words "well red" come into my head. Feeling a bit silly, I spoke out the word to her, saying, "I think the Lord is saying to you that you are well red." A few people laughed at that point, but the girl burst into tears. Mike indicated that I should go over and pray for her.

When she had recovered a bit, I asked her what the words meant to her. She explained that she was at university and studying English Literature. When I had spoken those words out, it meant two things to her. First, she took the words "well red" (well read) to refer to her knowledge of classical literature, showing that Jesus knew her, knew what she was studying and knew that she had read many books.

A second meaning of the word helped her in her current situation. She had been feeling very stressed as she had some very important exams the following week and was worried that she hadn't studied enough or covered everything. As she heard the words spoken out she knew that Jesus was affirming her and encouraging her that she had read *enough* – she was "well read"! Her anxiety and stress vanished and she felt full of joy and peace. This really amazed me. Through just two words God had done such a lot in such a short space of time.

Just two words may be enough in prophecy. We should never add to what we are given, otherwise we may change the whole meaning and not deliver what God intended at all. Isn't it amazing how God works? He doesn't need us, but He delights in involving us in what He is doing.

IN MY DREAMS!

For God does speak – now one way, now another – though no one perceives it. In a dream, in a vision of the night, when deep sleep falls on people as they slumber in their beds...

Job 33:14–15

I remember once dreaming about a friend of mine and his wife, who I had not seen for a while. In the dream there was a woman called Prudence. The dream was very vivid and when I awoke I wrote the dream down. I didn't know what the word "prudence" really meant, so I decided to look it up in a dictionary to get the full meaning. Then I looked it up in the Bible using a concordance. I prayed and asked the Holy Spirit for the interpretation of the dream and then I wrote down what I sensed the Holy Spirit had said.

I put the pieces of paper in an envelope and placed them in my bedside drawer. I knew the Lord would prompt me when it was the right time to send off this word to my friend. Sure enough, the Holy Spirit did prompt me about six months later, as *three* times in a day I remembered the prophecy and felt an urgency to send it off. After I sent it I heard nothing back from my friend for weeks and I felt quite anxious about that. But I decided to trust God with it and put it out of my mind.

About five months later, we happened to meet up and I asked him what he had thought about the dream. "Oh, I'm sorry," he said. "I forgot to let you know. It really meant a lot and was just the wake-up call I needed. I sorted out what was indicated in the dream and things are so much better now."

Phew! My relief was enormous.

WHat to DO WItH a DReam

If you have a spiritual dream given to you by God, it will not go away. In fact, it will get stronger throughout the day unless you ask God about it. Write down the important elements of the dream. Is there someone there representing authority? Are there any feelings in the dream? What are they? Were there any words of Scripture? If so, look them up and include them as well. Often the Scripture is a confirmation of the essence of the dream.

After writing out the dream, re-read it and ask the Holy Spirit what is significant about the different parts of it. Let Him speak to you, listening carefully for Him to speak out the interpretation and what it means for the person concerned. Finally, consider the application. In other words, how does it apply to the person?

We have to be very careful when interpreting dreams. They are not always clear and we will need to be wise in how we give out words about them.

BE Patient

I have much more to say to you, more than you can now bear.

John 16:12

These are the words of Jesus, spoken to the disciples before He ascended into heaven and the Holy Spirit came. Sometimes we have to wait until we have permission from the Lord to give a prophetic word. There often is a *right* time and a *wrong* time. Don't be hasty to give a word to someone. God may want you to hold it for some time, as I did with my "prudence" dream. Don't worry that the Holy Spirit will forget it is there. He will tell you loud and clear when to share it.

I need to say that after reading all of the above, I do not wish to sound as if I get prophecies every day and have regular prophetic dreams. For me, prophecies usually occur during prayer ministry. Significant dreams probably occur about four or five times a year. The more prayer ministry I do, the more I hear God and see Him working. The times when I ask Him, "Do you want to say something, Lord?" I usually hear Him speak. My expectation to hear God for others is high because I do it a lot. If you only make yourself available *sometimes* to God, then you will probably hear Him speak *sometimes*. If you make yourself available to God to hear Him speak *many times*, then I suggest you may hear Him speak *many times*.

HOW OFTEN SHOULD I PROPHESY AND WHERE SHOULD I DO IT?

As I have said previously, practise often in small groups because it is a brilliant way of learning in a safe environment alongside people who love you.

If you give out a prophecy in a church service or a public place, the Bible tells us that after three have been given the congregation should weigh what is being said, so expect to be led this way. The leaders will discern whether a prophecy is from God or not according to the Holy Spirit's confirmation.

Speaking out in a public place can be a scary thing to do and sometimes the Holy Spirit will give us a sign that He wants us to do just that. He wants us to speak words that He is giving us and He will anoint us to do it.

PHYSICAL RESPONSES TO BE AWARE OF

When the Holy Spirit wants to use me to prophesy, my body will often respond to the call in involuntary ways. I do not worry about this – in fact, just the opposite, as I know that God is active in and around me.

These are some of the signs I get or used to get, usually one or two of these at the same time:

- My heart begins to beat very fast. So fast, in fact, that I think I might die if I do not speak out the word!
- I can feel a heat on my back before I prophesy.
- Sometimes I am aware of feeling something huge in the pit of my stomach.
- My mouth tingles.
- I hear words in my thoughts when I am praying for people that I recognize as the voice of God.

It is good to identify what happens to our bodies when the Holy Spirit is present. Then we can recognize and be familiar with His presence and ask Him how He wants us to respond. Sometimes these manifestations happen when we first start using the gift. In time they may disappear. This doesn't mean that the gifting has gone. It may mean that you don't need that same encouragement to step out any more.

FINALLY, IT'S NOT ABOUT ME

The honour and glory goes to Jesus for everything He does and says. We need to always thank the Holy Spirit for His gift of prophecy so that we don't take the glory that is meant for Him. We must always remember that our motive in prophesying should be one of love, bringing others closer to Jesus and building up the church.

PRAYER

What a wonderful gift, Jesus – it sounds so exciting.
You said You want me to eagerly desire it, so I do.
Please teach me by using people to give me a word
of encouragement, strength or comfort from You.
Show me how You will use this gift through me. I offer
myself to You for You to use me in any way You want.
I know that You can use anyone to prophesy. Speak,
Lord – Your servant is listening. Amen.

SCRIPTURES

*If I have the gift of prophecy and can fathom all
mysteries and all knowledge, and if I have a faith that
can move mountains, but do not have love, I am nothing.*
1 Corinthians 13:2

In the last days, God says, I will pour out my Spirit on all people. Your sons and daughters will prophesy, your young men will see visions, your old men will dream dreams. Even on my servants, both men and women, I will pour out my Spirit in those days, and they will prophesy.

Acts 2:17–18

Two or three prophets should speak, and the others should weigh carefully what is said. And if a revelation comes to someone who is sitting down, the first speaker should stop. For you can all prophesy in turn so that everyone may be instructed and encouraged. The spirits of prophets are subject to the control of prophets. For God is not a God of disorder but of peace – as in all the congregations of the Lord's people.

1 Corinthians 14:29–33

Do not treat prophecies with contempt...

1 Thessalonians 5:20

Love never fails. But where there are prophecies, they will cease; where there are tongues, they will be stilled; where there is knowledge, it will pass away. For we know in part and we prophesy in part, but when completeness comes, what is in part disappears. When I was a child, I talked like a child, I thought like a child, I reasoned like a child. When I became a man, I put the ways of childhood behind me.

1 Corinthians 13:8–11

CHAPTER 10

. . . .

THE GIFT OF MIRACLES

... to another miraculous powers.

1 Corinthians 12:10

In this chapter, you will read many stories of different miracles that I have been privileged to see or hear about during the years I have been a Christian. Personally, I do not operate in the gift of miracles, but I wish I did, because I want to see people encounter Jesus and fall at His feet. One day, maybe!

It is God who gives the gift of miracles and it is God who gets the glory when they happen, so all the stories here are told to lift up *His* name and encourage us to be expectant for *more*!

WHAT IS A MIRACLE?

A miracle is a supernatural event contrary to the laws of nature. It is something that happens "out of the ordinary" and usually over a very short space of time. The Bible is full of miracles and in the gospels they seem to happen on a daily basis!

In the Old Testament we can read the miracles of the creation of the world, the shutting of hungry lions' mouths, the parting of seas and rivers, rancid water made sweet, city walls falling down at the sound of a trumpet blast, a floating axe-head and water flowing out of rocks. In the New Testament the miracles include a virgin birth, resurrections, walking on water, food provision for thousands, blind men seeing again, the deaf hearing, the paralysed walking, locked doors opening and chains being loosed.

Throughout the Bible, miracles display the magnificence of God, and Jesus would often use them as visual aids to teach more about the wonderful kingdom of God. The miracles of Jesus affirmed that what He was teaching was from God. Out of His compassion, Jesus answered the cries of the desperate, turning their worlds around for ever.

WHY DO WE SEE SO FEW MIRACLES TODAY?

Our experience of the miraculous seems to depend on where we live and the nature of our circumstances. In the West, we do not tend to suffer the terrible persecution that some Christians suffer in other parts of the world. They often seem to have access to miracles in order that the worship of Jesus can continue under regimes that oppose Him, since God will always find ways to encourage and strengthen His church, regardless of who tries to oppress it.

WE ARE NOT HUNGRY ENOUGH

In the UK, at least, I do not think we are hungry enough for God. It is so easy to rely on other sources to meet our needs and desires rather than letting our heavenly Father supply them. In a lot of other countries, people are desperate for so much and do not have, for instance, the good healthcare that we have in the West. How much easier is it for them to reach out to God for a miracle?

we Do noT Believe

In the gospel of Mark, Jesus tells a man that everything is possible for him who believes. The man answers Jesus:

I do believe; help me overcome my unbelief!

Mark 9:24

On another occasion, Jesus pointed out to the disciples that their unbelief was getting in the way, and He told them to fast and pray.

Do we believe that miracles are only for Bible times, or do we believe that they can and do happen today, even through us? God can, of course, perform miracles through a sovereign act whenever and however He wants to, but do we believe He can use us? Does He actually *want* to?

The answer is simple: Yes!

Let me remind you of what Jesus said to His disciples:

Very truly I tell you, whoever believes in me will do the works I have been doing, and they will do even greater things than these, because I am going to the Father.

John 14:12

We simply need to believe His promise.

IT IS TIme To eHPecT mIRacLeS!

I have to admit that when I first became a Christian I was bursting with hunger and expectancy that I would see miracles. I remember reading stories of Smith Wigglesworth praying for people, and how their wooden stumps grew into new limbs, and I hardly blinked because it was what I expected God to do. Many years later, when I read the same book again I was gasping at the stories. It saddened me that over the years I had lost something:

my expectancy. When I had become a Christian all those years ago, I was very broken and needed supernatural healing on a daily basis. God was so near to me and I could feel His healing power changing me and making me new. But I had become familiar with it, and I realized I needed to say sorry that I had lost my simple faith in His ability to do the miraculous.

Are you in the same place I was? Do you need God to refresh you with a new expectancy for miracles? Why don't you say this prayer with me?

> Dear Jesus, I am sorry that I seem to have so little
> expectancy of You doing a miracle through me.
> Forgive me for thinking that You would never use
> me to do such a thing. I want to see miracles, Lord!
> I want to see them in my family and in my church. I
> want to see them on the streets, so that Your kingdom
> is extended and that people will see how wonderful
> You are. I do believe; help me overcome my unbelief!
> I offer myself to You. Fill me now, Holy Spirit, with
> expectancy and eyes to see. Surprise me, Lord! Give
> me opportunities to see You work in this way and give
> me boldness and courage to take a step of faith in
> seeing the miraculous happen around me. Release
> people in my church with a gift of miracles. I ask this
> to glorify You, Lord Jesus. Amen.

WHO HAS the GLORY?

When men and women operate in the gift of miracles there is a real temptation to put them on a pedestal. God does not want us to do that. The gift of miracles is a gift like all the others and its purpose is to point us to the Giver of the gift, not the person who has it. God does not choose special people to receive it, but He does choose people who He knows can steward it well. It may look as if it is an easy gift to have, but it is not. It requires dedication and total commitment. Jesus said:

From everyone who has been given much, much will be demanded; and from the one who has been entrusted with much, much more will be asked.

Luke 12:48

So rather than exalting people who have the gift of miracles, we must pray for them to stay close to the Lord and ask Him to increase this gift to bless our church and community.

Time to testify

The Bible speaks about the power of the "word of testimony" in defeating the enemy:

They triumphed over him by the blood of the Lamb and by the word of their testimony...

Revelation 12:11

The following stories are testimonies of modern-day miracles which will encourage and inspire you, leaving you, I hope, expectant for more. I have changed the names to protect identities.

ROB'S FINGER

In the early days after our own "Pentecost" experience at St Andrew's Church, many of us were very keen to continue ministering healing to one another. One day, there was a knock at our door and our neighbour Rob was standing on our doorstep holding a cloth round his hand, blood pouring from one of his fingers. I do not like the sight of blood at all, especially in large quantities such as this. Rob quickly explained that he had cut himself with a chain-saw and rather than go directly to A&E at the local hospital, he thought it would be a great opportunity for a miracle!

Although I admired his courage, my thoughts steered to the beautiful off-white carpet we had recently had fitted in our lounge! I called out to my husband, who quickly rang another couple of friends from church to come and pray with us for Rob. As Rob removed the covering over his finger I nearly passed out. The cut was jagged and very, very deep. In fact, I was sure I could see the bone. We started to pray, holding our hands over his finger, and kept speaking healing to it in Jesus' name. The most incredible thing started to happen before our eyes. Within half an hour we watched the skin coming completely together and the bleeding stopped!

The whole experience, although exciting, left us all feeling a bit shocked. To be honest, at the beginning, the faith for the task belonged to Rob. He wanted his miracle and he received it! We, on the other hand, began with little faith but saw it increase as time progressed and we continued to pray together. Although we witnessed a miracle, it was confusing when a week later we heard that Rob had to have antibiotics, as his finger had become infected. We continued to praise God for what we had seen and realized that we should have met with Rob a few more times until the finger was completely healed. Nevertheless, it was a huge boost to our expectancy to pray for others.

BETH'S HAND AND THE SAAB

When our daughter Beth was almost two, I took her in the family car down to our local village. At that time we had a Saab which had strong steel reinforcements inserted in the doors for added protection. As a result of the steel being there, the doors were very heavy and to close one required some strength to really slam the door.

When we arrived in the village I parked the car and lifted Beth out of her child seat in the back of the car. Opening the passenger door, I then retrieved my handbag. When I slammed the door to shut it I was horrified to see Beth's hand trapped inside! She cried out in pain and I shouted out, "Jesus, help me!"

Feeling sick and faint, I opened up the door and for some reason automatically shoved her little hand under my armpit, as if that would cure it! I ran across the road towards the children's clothes shop, all the while aware that Beth was not making any sound. I rushed into the shop and immediately sat down on a chair by the front door. I was praying all the while in tongues and still had Beth's arm under my armpit. I breathlessly explained to the shop assistant what had just happened and she went quickly to get a cold, wet cloth.

I decided to have a look at Beth's hand and very carefully I removed it from under my armpit. All that could be seen was a faint red line across her hand! I was shocked and amazed. The shop assistant returned with the cloth and looked at Beth's hand. Like me, she was completely flabbergasted by the lack of blood.

Later on I decided to examine the car door and saw that the locks on those doors really were enormous and their large prongs would certainly cause a serious injury if a hand was caught in them. The enormity of what had taken place earlier in the day really hit me and I worshipped the living God who had saved my little girl's hand from being mangled.

Sometimes, when I would tell people this story, they would not believe it. I would be amazed how people would dumb down what had happened, explaining away our miracle with comments such as, "Well, babies' hands are very soft and bendy" or "She probably got it caught in a space" or even "The door probably didn't shut properly."

I know what happened. I know I saw Jesus perform a miracle that day.

ALEX'S RING IN THE SAND

When our eldest daughter, Alex, was about nine years old, we travelled with a group from our church to a beachside campsite in France. A few of us were chilling in our caravan when Alex came running in shouting out, "I dropped my ring in the sand! Please come and find it with me!" My heart sank as I realized that the little silver ring, our daughter's prized possession, had now become someone else's buried treasure.

Before we went to find it, to my surprise Alex said, "Come on, Daddy, let's pray and ask Jesus. He knows where it is." At that moment, like many other parents, I am sure, we prayed without very much faith at all. I doubt that we even had as much as a grain of mustard seed, but we prayed together for Jesus to show us where the ring was.

Following her out to the beach that stretched for as far as the eye could see in both directions, we asked her to show us where she had been playing. As we expected, she had no idea. So we walked quite a way along the beach and, taking a deep breath, my husband plunged his hand into the sand. His hand came up out of the sand clutching the silver ring, gleaming in the sunshine on the end of his little finger! We both stood there with our mouths wide open.

Was Alex surprised? Not a bit! "Thank you, Jesus!" she shouted as she lifted the ring off her Daddy's finger and slipped it onto her own. To be honest, we spent the rest of the day in a daze. Jesus said that we should become as little children and we would see the kingdom of heaven – and it turns out He was right!

THE LOST KEYS AND THE ANGEL

One of the hazards of praying with your children and telling them that Jesus works miracles is that they very easily expect them to happen and expect their parents to have as big a faith and expectancy as they have themselves. When one of our children was young I mislaid my bunch of keys. I had looked in all the usual places and walked into every room, passing through the hallway several times. My daughter Beth suddenly said, "Mummy, let's ask Jesus to send an angel to put them where we can see them." "Good idea!" I thought. I prayed out loud with Beth and we said a big "Amen!" together.

I felt compelled to walk into the hallway, and there they were, sitting on the seat of Beth's trike. I let out a gasp of surprise, as I *knew* they had not been there earlier. I had been through that hallway several times and I had only taken the trike out there five minutes previously. Of course, Beth wasn't at all surprised, as she had believed 100 per cent that an angel would visit us that day.

MY HAND AND THE CHEST FREEZER

Years ago the first type of freezers that people had in their homes were called chest freezers. They were huge with a big lid and were large enough to freeze a chopped-up cow! (Actually, we did once buy half a cow, as it was a lot cheaper that way.) Anyway, as time went on this fashion faded and freezers upgraded in design and size, which meant that most of the time half our freezer remained empty and all of the frozen food would occupy the lower half of the freezer. Retrieving the food was not a problem for most people, but being only five feet two inches, I could not reach to the bottom very easily at all.

One day, I was half falling into the freezer, trying to reach something, and as I crawled out, my hand slipped. The heavy lid came crashing down on my other hand that was holding two lamb chops still partly inside the freezer. The lid had two sharp prongs on it designed, for some reason, so that we could lock it. I screamed out as I felt the prongs pierce the back of my hand.

Without thinking, I shouted out, "Jesus, heal me!" I removed my hand, frightened to look – remember, I hate the sight of blood. To my amazement all that could be seen were two very faint pink lines where I had felt the prongs pierce me. Amazing! Praise God for another miracle.

A ReSCUING aNGeL

At one time my husband and I were converting an old coach into a coffee bus for the gang of young people that hung about the streets in our village. It had taken us a long time. We had decided to completely strip the interior, as the coverings on the ceiling and seats were really smelly. Through a mutual friend, I was given a contact who had a supply of thick foam, suitable for re-covering the seats. This man lived in a town about fifteen miles away. It was in the days before mobile phones, so I arranged to meet him at a particular spot in the oldest part of the town. When I reached the spot I was frustrated to see that local festivities were taking place. There were crowds of people gathered to watch morris dancers and I had no idea how I was going to find this man in the mayhem, since I had no idea what he looked like.

I spotted a sign that said "Enquiries", so I walked towards that building which, from the outside, looked open. When I stepped inside, however, I discovered that all the small shops were shut. I felt disappointed, as I had hoped that the man I was meeting would have been waiting in this building for me, away from the crowds.

As I walked out of the building, I nearly crashed into someone walking by. Apologizing, I heard the man say, "Are you looking for John Williams?" I replied that I was and asked if he knew where I could find him. The stranger pointed to a pub on the other side of the road and asked if he could go and get John for me. I told him that would be great, so the man crossed over the road and entered the pub. A short time later, out came John Williams and I greeted him, saying how amazing it was that his friend met me and knew where he was. John looked puzzled and said, "What friend?" I explained about the man with the beard that I'd bumped into and what he had said. John said, "That wasn't my friend. I have never seen him before in my life!" Hearing this made all the hairs stand up on the back of my neck. I decided that this man must have been an angel, as there seemed no other explanation. John and I went off to the warehouse where he showed me tons of thick foam, which was perfect for the re-upholstering of the bus seating. On the way home I felt in awe of God that He should send an angel to help me in this way. It seemed in some ways bizarre that Almighty God would be interested in helping me to get foam for a bus. However, it confirmed to me again that God was interested in what we were trying to set up for the young people, and that He was prepared to do a miracle to show us that He would provide all of our needs. And He did! Thank you, Jesus.

A DEAF EAR

Once I prayed for a young woman called Chloe who needed emotional healing. Jesus answered our prayers and she had a deep encounter with the Holy Spirit, which was wonderful. At the end of the time, I asked her if she wanted prayer for anything else and she asked if I would pray for healing, as she had been deaf in one ear since birth. My first thought was that I would have preferred to pray for a headache to be healed rather than a deaf ear, but I asked the Holy Spirit to come upon her afresh anyway, knowing He loves to heal and nothing is too difficult for God.

After a while I suddenly remembered the time when Jesus put His finger into a deaf man's ear and told it to open. To be honest, at the time I had no thought about what I was doing but decided to follow this prompting from the Holy Spirit. I gently placed my finger in Chloe's ear and said out loud, "In the name of Jesus Christ I tell this ear to be opened and to hear."

I removed my finger, giving no thought at the time to ear wax – that came later! All I wanted was for her to hear – I was just trying to be obedient to God. Straight after I had removed my finger from her ear, she said quite calmly, "I can hear now."

Very shocked, I said, "Pardon?" I had not expected her to be healed at all!

My next thought was that I had better test out what she was saying, so I asked her to put her finger in her other ear and said that I would whisper something in the previously deaf ear.

To my astonishment, she repeated what I had just whispered. She seemed to be very accepting and although she was smiling, she didn't seem to be at all surprised about what had happened. We thanked Jesus and parted. I was on a high for about a week afterwards. Praise God!

Some of these stories happened many years ago and even though they will always be special, I want to share some that are really fresh and up to date. The following miracles happened while some young people were doing the praying and, for some of the group, it was the first time they had ever ministered in this way.

A SMORGASBORD OF RECENT MIRACLES

At a seminar recently, I was speaking on physical and emotional healing. A couple of hundred young people were standing waiting upon the Holy Spirit, asking Him for words of knowledge. They wanted to know about physical or emotional conditions that needed healing. Before anyone had spoken out any words, a young woman cried out and rushed to the front saying, "My ankle is healed! As I stood up, suddenly all the pain had gone. I have been suffering from a bad injury and it was difficult to move and now it is healed!" We all cheered, clapped and thanked Jesus.

During the following half an hour at the same seminar some fifteen more people were miraculously healed. Those who had laid hands on them were mostly young people, unused to ministering in this way. Here are some of the quick-fire testimonies of people who came to the microphone to say they had been healed.

A teenage boy was healed of dyslexia. He read an A4 page of typing at speed and was able to recite it all correctly without transposing any words.

A woman who had had tuberculosis for twenty-two years and could only take shallow breaths as a result, was suddenly able to expand her lungs fully and breathe normally.

A young teenage girl who had had a painful earache on and off for two years suddenly heard a "pop" in her ear, and all the pain had gone. She could now hear clearly.

AN INNER HEALING MIRACLE

A young woman approached me on the last night of a Soul Survivor Festival and asked me to pray for her. She told me that five years previously, two men had raped her. She had never told anyone about this until a couple of months before, when she went to see a counsellor. Two years after the initial assault, her boyfriend also abused her. I was very conscious of the fact that this was the last night of the Festival and she had only just plucked up her courage to ask for prayer. Although humanly speaking I wanted her to receive a major healing, I knew that this sort of freedom often took time, as the pain was very deep. I asked her if she was feeling any pain in her body as I prayed. She confirmed that she had some pain in her stomach, so I asked her if I could place my hand there. As I was remaining open to the Holy Spirit, He reminded me of several times when Jesus spoke to women who had suffered. I then spoke this over her:

"Jesus met women who had suffered pain, and just as He said to them, He is now saying to you, be free from your suffering. Be free from your suffering in Jesus' name."

Immediately she cried out, "It's gone – all the pain has gone!" Her face was radiant. She jumped up and was delighted at the miraculous release from her pain. It was a joy to watch what Jesus did. As always, I knew that I had done nothing – it was all Him. Glory to His name!

LET YOUR FAITH RISE!

All the stories I have told are shared to excite you afresh about our God. Yes, He does heal today! Yes, He does do miracles!

If you see miracles, keep a journal of them. Write down everything you see, hear and experience, because there is power in the testimony. When you need encouragement, a fresh filling of hope or faith, take out the journal and re-read the testimonies.

They will not only bless you, but they will keep you hungry and expectant to see the Lord do more.

My last story here is a personal one. It does not involve anyone laying hands on me using the gift of miracles, but I tell it to honour Jesus by showing that He does not *need* to use us, but He *chooses* to.

In my previous book, *Let the Healing Begin* (Kingsway, 2007), I told my testimony of how I got to know Jesus. It includes this story of miraculous healing.

Our firstborn child was stillborn. Her brain had not developed properly in the womb and she was unable to sustain life. In hospital in those days, mothers were not allowed to see their stillborn babies and, as in our case, did not even know where their baby was buried. As we were being told by the doctor that our baby had died, a sheet was being thrown over her. In my mind I thought that she must have looked horrific, with a deformed head or something, as I wasn't allowed to see her. Perhaps the doctors thought that they were protecting the parents, but it actually made the suffering worse. I deliberately closed my mind to all thoughts of our child. This meant that I did not grieve and I continued in this state for seven years. I never cried over her, but just felt a dull ache inside most of the time. In my head, I felt that I had done a terrible thing in giving birth to a "thing", something deformed. There was no funeral and we never even gave our child a name. All we knew was that she was a little girl, but we had no idea where the hospital had taken her. This meant that we had never mentioned our baby to our other children born after her.

Our daughter, Alex, was about five years old and I was driving along a country lane when she suddenly asked, "Mummy, was I your first baby?" I nearly crashed the car into the bank. Where did that question come from? She asked again, "Did you have another baby before me?"

I replied, "Yes, darling, I did. I had a little girl, but she couldn't live."

Undeterred, Alex excitedly asked what her name was; what had we called her? Suddenly, I felt as if two halves of my brain clicked together and I uttered the name I had never previously called her: "Sarah. Her name is Sarah."

Alex was full of excitement now. "Sarah. My sister is called Sarah. I bet she is having a lovely time with Jesus now, Mummy..." And off she went, chattering for the rest of the journey about her sister in heaven.

When I uttered Sarah's name I was instantly healed of all the grief stored up inside me. I was filled with joy at the thought of Sarah, my child. When I got home I told my husband what had happened. For the next few weeks I brought Sarah into conversations with my friends and family as I embraced her again and again, seeing her in her rightful place. She was and is part of our family. For me, this was a miracle. Seven years of misplaced grieving suddenly healed in a moment. Only Jesus could do stuff like that!

I offer all these stories to the glory of God. He did them – no one else but Him.

PRAYER

Jesus, I love reading about Your miracles. Increase my expectation, Holy Spirit, of seeing You doing miracles in my life and in those around me. Thank You that You are not limited by my lack of understanding. Please release the gift of miracles in my church. Show me how to love people like You do. I want to see You act in this way so that many people will come to know You. Surprise me by letting me see this gift in action. Fill me with Your compassion for a hurting world. Thank You, Lord. Amen.

ACTION

Our God is a miracle worker, a miracle maker. Nothing is impossible for Him. Nothing. He is not restricted to the laws of physics. He is above all that. Nothing that has ever happened to you, no pain from abuse or sickness or abandonment is too complex for God to heal with a miracle.

What miracle would you ask God for right now?

Begin to reach out in faith as you pray for that miracle.

SCRIPTURES

References for some miracles of Jesus:

- Jesus walks on water (Matthew 14:22–33).
- Blind Bartimaeus receives sight (Mark 10:46–52).
- Thousands are fed (Matthew 14:15–21).
- A widow's son is raised (Luke 7:11–17).
- A centurion's servant is healed (Luke 7:1–10).
- Jesus turns water into wine (John 2:1–11).
- Ten lepers are healed (Luke 17:11–19).
- Lazarus is raised from the dead (John 11:1–45).
- A miraculous catch of fish (John 21:1–14).
- Jesus restores a man's severed ear (Luke 22:49–51).
- Jesus calms a storm (Matthew 8:23–27).

CHAPTER 11

························

GIFTS OF HEALING

I am the Lord, who heals you.

Exodus 15:26

In the gospels we read how Jesus healed many people, completely turning their lives around. The great news is that Jesus still heals today, and in this chapter I will be telling some stories of what I have seen and experienced myself.

The first time I was healed was when I was a baby. I had suffered a big blow to my head in an accident, and then a couple of weeks later I banged my head again. The second one was not as severe as the first, but it caused me to have a delayed concussion. It was my auntie who noticed that instead of sleeping peacefully in my cot, I was foaming at the mouth! So I was rushed to the hospital by ambulance and apparently, at the time, the outlook was so bad that I was given the last rites by the hospital priest, who sat by my bedside praying all night. Obviously, I recovered and am here to tell the tale! That was the first of many major healings that have taken place in my life, physically, mentally, emotionally and spiritually.

Have you ever been healed? Have you ever had a cold? Did you get better? Did you die, only to be raised from the dead? Some people are! Do you know that it is no more difficult for Jesus to raise the dead than to cure a cold? Nor is it any more difficult for Him to shrink and destroy a brain tumour than it is to heal a headache. Nothing is impossible for God. The main obstacle to receiving healing is found in us. Our perception, expectation, hope and belief in healing all need to come into line with what the Bible says and what Jesus modelled during His three years of earthly ministry. Healing is a process. Sometimes we may become disappointed as we pray for healing, as our expectation is for a miracle. A miraculous healing is instant. Healing often happens after praying more than once or can happen a while after we have prayed.

WHat causes sickness?

Sickness and disease were not created by God and His design and destiny for us was, and still is, that we live in full health. I do not pretend to know all of the answers to what causes sickness but here are some of my thoughts:

- It may be that we become ill because the enemy is afflicting us with something.
- It may be as a result of living a harmful or sinful lifestyle in which we abuse our bodies.
- It may be that we have sinned against someone or are harbouring unforgiveness or bitterness.
- Other people may have done us harm and we have become sick as a by-product. Negative emotions can affect our physical health.
- Sometimes our bodies feel worn out through age and we find it more difficult to fight infection.
- It may be that we are living in the legacy of man's original sin seen in Genesis.
- Often we don't know why.

Whatever the reason, our destiny as seen in Scripture is that we are to live life in all its fullness, so it is important that whenever possible we choose health.

OUR amazing Bodies

Normally, when we have a physical ailment, the body heals itself. God created us that way. Our bodies are continually being restored and made new by an amazing and complex system of cell re-growth and defence mechanisms. In Psalm 139 we read:

For you created my inmost being; you knit me together in my mother's womb. I praise you because I am fearfully and wonderfully made; your works are wonderful, I know that full well.

Psalm 139:13–14

Start looking at how we are put together and how it all works, and I am sure you will agree. So much of our body is being renewed day by day. For example, nails grow and hair falls out to make room for new growth. Mostly it just happens without us needing to do anything about it.

If I was unwell when I was younger, I imagined that little soldiers were fighting the infection that was invading my body. In some ways that was true. We are designed in such a way that our bodies activate an inbuilt resistance army of white cells that continually fight anything that has come to steal our health. Most of the time we are totally unaware that the battle is taking place.

Healing Gifts

... to another gifts of healing by that one Spirit...

1 Corinthians 12:9

The subject of healing is enormous. I could not possibly cover it all in just one chapter of a book, but my aim is to give you a simple introduction to what this gift is and how we can use it.

First of all, notice in the verse above that the word "gifts" is plural. The Holy Spirit imparts "gifts of healing". In other words, the Holy Spirit has more than one way of healing people and we should expect that He will use us in many different ways to minister to those who need healing.

Healing is, of course, not just physical. We are told in the Bible that:

Jesus went through all the towns and villages, teaching in their synagogues, proclaiming the good news of the kingdom and healing every disease and sickness.

Matthew 9:35

Jesus offered freedom from every kind of physical, emotional, mental and spiritual affliction. His healing was holistic, for the complete person. I am passionate about seeing healing come to the broken-hearted and those suffering emotional pain. This does not mean that I ignore those who are suffering physically, it just means that I mainly operate in the area of emotional healing. I have been privileged to see many people receive their physical healing during ministry times, but when I pray for people, I am concerned for their *complete* wholeness.

JESUS IN PARTNERSHIP

Jesus was anointed to heal the sick, but He only did it once He knew what the Father was doing:

Jesus gave them this answer: "Very truly I tell you, the Son can do nothing by himself; he can do only what he sees his Father doing, because whatever the Father does the Son also does."

John 5:19

When we receive the gifts of healing from the Holy Spirit we must use them in the same way. They are not gifts given to make us look good, and they should not be used inappropriately. Like Jesus, we use the gifts of healing from a foundation of humility and compassion. I am sure that you have seen images of over-zealous preachers who seem more interested in "performance ministry" than being humble, compassionate channels through which the love of Jesus can flow. Let us choose to do it differently, in partnership with the Holy Spirit.

Preparation time

We read so often in Scripture how Jesus was moved with compassion before healing someone. In the same way, we need love and compassion when we pray for people for healing, as it is in this atmosphere that the miracles will happen.

Join me now in asking the Holy Spirit to fill us with the love of Jesus for those who need healing:

> Dear Holy Spirit, please fill me with the compassion
> of Jesus for people who are hurting or broken.
> Please give me eyes to see what Jesus sees. I do not
> want to get distracted by analyzing their condition,
> because You are the Healer, not me. I want to really
> love people from my heart, letting You lead me, and
> I want to see people made whole. Use me to bring
> Your kingdom into people's lives. I want to glorify Your
> name from a place of humility and obedience. Amen.

Before we begin praying for others, we need to open up ourselves to the Holy Spirit, inviting Him to anoint us with power and asking Him to make us clean. Healing is always God's work, never ours, and He must receive all the glory for every single healing, large or small. So it is important that we do away with any fleshly pride before we start.

After seeing someone healed we can get an amazing feeling of elation, wonder and awe. It is very important that we remember to guard ourselves from spiritual pride here too. Pride is an ugly thing and the enemy likes nothing better than to puff up our egos when things go well. Be on your guard.

Likewise, when nothing much seems to be happening as we pray for people to be healed, the enemy will whisper that it is our fault, that we are useless and should stop doing it. Reject those lies! It is God who heals and He wants to use *you* in partnership with Him to do it.

HOW DID JESUS HEAL?

Jesus' earthly ministry was all about telling people what the kingdom of God is like. Amongst other things, this involved freedom from sickness and deliverance from evil spirits. Initially, He started modelling this while His disciples watched and after a while, He did it with them, encouraging them to copy Him. Finally, He sent them out in pairs in His name to do these things without Him.

At the beginning of His ministry, soon after He had been baptized in the river Jordan and had come out of the desert, full of the Holy Spirit, he entered a synagogue and read out a passage from Isaiah. Here are the words He spoke out, with my comments inserted:

... the scroll of the prophet Isaiah was handed to [Jesus]. Unrolling it, he found the place where it is written:
"The Spirit of the Lord [the Holy Spirit] is on me, because he has anointed me [set apart for a special purpose] to proclaim good news [salvation] to the poor. He has sent me to proclaim freedom for the prisoners [those imprisoned by emotional and mental sickness] and recovery of sight for the blind [those with physical sickness and disease], to set the oppressed free [the bereaved and depressed], to

161

proclaim the year of the Lord's favor."

Then he rolled up the scroll, gave it back to the attendant and sat down. The eyes of everyone in the synagogue were fastened on him. He began by saying to them, "Today this scripture is fulfilled in your hearing."

Luke 4:17–21

Jesus had come to fulfil that prophecy. The origin of these verses is Isaiah 61:1–2. This passage covers grief, loss and mourning in more detail. This piece of Scripture was like Jesus' manifesto. He read out what He was going to do through His life and work before He did it, unlike some politicians today, who give us their manifesto and then ignore it! Jesus was different: He did what He promised He would do.

The good news is, Jesus hasn't stopped doing it! Not only that, He will continue doing it through the church, you and me, until He comes again, when there will be no more sorrow or sickness. Jesus loves making people whole.

He would often ask people, "What do you want Me to do for you?" because they would then engage with Him relationally around their healing. Jesus would never presume a person wanted to be healed; it was always done with permission and out of choice. The same is true today. Some may have had a physical disability for a long time and they may have given up hope of healing. We need to pray for whatever the person is asking for in prayer, while keeping open to what the Holy Spirit may be saying regarding the disability.

Jesus knew that there was a possibility that some people may not actually *want* to be healed because their disease had become their identity. Sickness can be a way of getting attention in prayer ministry. When Jesus heals, the person no longer has a vehicle for special treatment from others to fill that emotional need. Others may have long-term illness and find it too hard or scary to take up the responsibilities of living a normal life. They don't feel that they could cope. We need to be both wise and compassionate in this instance. It is good to follow the example of Jesus and ask the same effective question as He did.

WHAT IS "WHOLENESS"?

The Greek word *sozo* means "to save" and implies wholeness. In the New Testament this word is used many times to describe what was happening when Jesus was healing people. The healing they received included body, soul and spirit.

You can do a study of this wonderful little word *sozo* by going online and putting it into a search engine. A *sozo* healing involves:

- Healing of the body from diseases, disabilities, ailments and infections.
- Healing of the heart from damaged emotions, past hurts, painful experiences, wrong choices and abuse.
- Healing of the spirit from bondages, curses, unforgiveness of self or of others, lies about who God is and lies about another person.
- Healing of the mind from depression, abuse and suicidal thoughts.

Many people need healing in more than one of these areas or even in all of them. When a person asks for prayer for healing, they may expect it to happen one way but often, Jesus heals something else first. Maybe, for instance, a spiritual healing needs taking care of before a physical one. It is important not to be disappointed when healing does not seem to happen the way we expect, and remember that God knows what He is doing.

There are many instances in the Bible when Jesus did not just heal a person's physical state, but healed the person spiritually or emotionally. Jesus was not just interested in the symptoms of a sickness but in the deeper things too. Think, for instance, of the paralysed man who was carried to Jesus on a stretcher by his friends:

> *Jesus stepped into a boat, crossed over and came to his*
> *own town. Some men brought to him a paralyzed man, lying*
> *on a mat. When Jesus saw their faith, he said to the man,*
> *"Take heart, son; your sins are forgiven."*
>
> **Matthew 9:1–2**

First of all Jesus called the man "son". This affirmed him and brought healing to him emotionally, as it gave him a sense of belonging and acceptance. Then Jesus told him that his sins were forgiven so that his spirit was healed. Finally, Jesus told him to stand up, take his mat and walk, which was the physical healing he had been hoping for all along. He just received more than he had bargained for!

There are many other stories from the Bible of Jesus healing on more than one level. Remember the woman healed from the issue of blood in Luke 8:43–48? She was not only healed of her physical ailment, but freed from shame and affirmed as a daughter in God's family. Wonderful!

Healing involves faith. Jesus looked to see if the one that needed healing had faith. Someone has to have it – either the person praying, the one being prayed for or friends who have brought the person to Jesus to be healed. It's not about big faith or little faith. Faith like a grain of mustard seed is all that is necessary. It is enough to move mountains. Faith is like a fuse wire that conducts the power of God to the place of need.

EXAMPLES OF PHYSICAL/EMOTIONAL HEALING

During a workshop I was leading recently, a man came forward in response to a word of knowledge given out for someone who had painful shoulders. The Holy Spirit told someone that this person had pain radiating out from a shoulder-blade. The man came up to the microphone after receiving prayer to say that, yes, he had been healed of all the shoulder pain, but an unexpected bonus was that the anxiety and fear he had been carrying because of his wife's illness had also been taken away. No one had prayed about that, but Jesus had taken it from him. He said that this meant more to him than the physical healing! The great thing was that the people who were praying for him had never prayed in this type of ministry before, so it meant that Jesus really did get all the glory for the healing.

This illustrates that we may pray for *physical healing* and find that *emotional healing* has taken place as a by-product. Sometimes, emotional sickness can actually be the cause of the physical sickness, so the heart needs healing first.

I remember once at a Soul Survivor festival, Mike Pilavachi gave out a word of knowledge for someone with a sore index finger. A man responded to this word and as we started to pray I distinctly sensed that he also had some distressing issues relating to his father, so I gently asked him about their relationship. At that point, a catalogue of memories and pain connected to his father was opened up. My husband and I spent the next couple of days meeting up with him as Jesus started to release the pain and bring healing. At the end of the time he made no mention of the finger that had been so painful. Either it had been healed or else it was inconsequential compared with the emotional healing he had received.

AMY'S STORY

At another festival some years ago, I met a youth leader in her thirties called Amy. This lady looked very unhappy, so I decided to ask her why. Amy told me that for the past year she had been seeing a psychiatrist because she had tried to take her own life by taking large amounts of pills and alcohol. Thankfully, she received excellent medical care and the doctors were able to save her.

Prior to her suicide attempt, she had had serious depression for ten years. As Amy talked, I asked the Holy Spirit why she was this way. Two words came into my mind by word of knowledge:

"Baby died". I had the impression that this word was about a tiny baby, so I asked Amy if she had any children and she told me she had two boys. I then asked her if the births had been difficult and she responded that they had not, but that ten years previously she had had another baby who died. At this point I knew that this was the root of her depression and I knew by the gift of faith that Jesus wanted to heal her.

Amy told me she had never grieved for her dead baby because she had had two friends at the time, both of whom had lost much older children, so she had felt that somehow their grief was worse than hers. She had felt that she needed to be strong for them, despite experiencing her own terrible grief. She had locked her grief away.

I was suddenly filled with the love and compassion of Jesus for Amy and I assured her that it was time for her to grieve now, so that Jesus could heal her. I asked Jesus for His healing love to come upon her and she began to sob for about five minutes until the grief seemed to drain away.

When she was more composed, I asked her the name of the baby who had died, but she told me the baby had never been given a name. I asked Jesus to give Amy a name for her baby and suddenly she began to smile as she savoured her baby's name. I continued to pray for her in tongues and then had a prophecy and a word of knowledge for her that her marriage would recover and be healed after years of strife. I encouraged her also to tell her other children about their little sister they had never known – they needed to talk about her and celebrate her as a family member.

When I saw Amy the next day, I saw a completely different woman! She looked radiant and free, nothing like the depressed person of the day before. She had been healed and ten years of pain had been lifted during one time of prayer.

Although Jesus could have done this for Amy on His own, He chose to use me as a catalyst. Because all of His gifts are available to us to use all of the time, He gave me more than one Holy Spirit gift to complete the job, as you will see from the story.

I thanked Him for using me and I want this story to encourage you that He wants to use you in the same way too.

RECEIVING THE GIFT OF HEALING

When you first receive gifts of healing you may be aware of tingling, heaviness or heat in your hands. This can be a sign that the Holy Spirit is anointing you with the gifts. Try not to be alarmed if this sign stops in time, as it does not mean that the gifts have gone away. Sometimes these signs are given early on to encourage us to step out and use the gifts. Do not get caught up in these mysterious symptoms, as it may become a stumbling block to you remaining open to the Holy Spirit. Actually, some people get no sign of their anointing at all, but are still used by the Holy Spirit. If you would like these particular gifts, just ask Jesus for them and have faith that He will answer you.

PRAYING FOR PEOPLE TO BE HEALED

PHYSICALLY

When I use the gifts of healing I do not get anxious that the person might not get healed immediately, because their healing is not my responsibility. That belongs to Jesus. It is His responsibility because the people are His children and not mine. So I do not fill my head with questions such as "What if they are not healed?" I leave that to the Lord. Also, I do not worry about letting God down when I pray for people. How can I possibly let Him down? He is God! All I try to do is to be obedient with what I sense He wants to do through me at any particular time. If He chooses to do things a different way from my way, that's absolutely fine. After all, His ways are always so much better than my ways (Isaiah 55:8–9).

Whenever we pray for healing, something always happens. It might not be what we expect, but people are always blessed by it. While you are praying for their physical healing, the person may feel heat or warmth in their body. This may be an indication that the Lord is at work, healing them. Others may feel the affected area getting cold where healing is needed, and the same applies. Not everyone who feels warmth or cold gets healed and people can get healed feeling nothing at all! Try not to get distracted by the manifestations, but focus on the presence of God.

Emotionally

As ministers of God's healing we are like the people who brought the paralysed man on the mat to Jesus. We too can carry expectant people to Jesus to be healed. We call on the name of Jesus, expecting Him to act, to heal, and to release freedom. We are effectively saying, "Use me, Lord, as a channel of the power of Your love. Let the light of Your love shine into darkness, let the oil of Your healing be poured out. Make me a channel of Your compassion. Let Your kingdom come, let Your will be done." All this is prayed in silence, inwardly acknowledging that God is at work. We are making ourselves available to the Holy Spirit, the One who brings the healing of Jesus. He wants not only to heal but also to involve us in the process.

Ministering God's love as part of prayer for healing is so important, especially for those who may have suffered abuse as children, physically or emotionally. They may have been neglected and may have never known what it is to experience real love. The wonderful thing is that Jesus, who is the same yesterday, today and forever, can visit the past and bring healing. People who have been abused can take a long while to allow the healing love of Jesus to come in and release their pain. They suffer not only intense pain, but usually find it difficult to trust anyone – even the One who just wants to heal them. We need to be sensitive to this and realize that it will be little by little that they allow this pain to surface.

I recently met a man at the end of a seminar entitled, "Getting Plugged Into The Holy Spirit". During the seminar he found himself breathing heavily and was aware of pain surfacing from his past. Most of the people had left, but I spotted this same man still seated. I walked over and asked him if he was OK. He said that he could not stand up – he was rooted to his chair.

Jesus often gives good visual aids. He obviously didn't want this man to leave the building until he had been healed and set free. The man (I will call him Peter) said that he had been sexually abused as a child and it had affected his life ever since.

I and another man started to minister the healing of Jesus to him. After waiting for the Holy Spirit to come upon him afresh, we asked Jesus to release the "little boy's pain" – to visit the little boy in his fear. Peter's heavy breathing increased. He was making a noise as if he was puffing out air. He started making groaning noises followed by coughing and retching.

Within a few minutes, however, he looked up and said he felt completely free – a great, heavy weight had lifted off him. He said that he had always felt unclean. I asked him if he still felt that. He said he wasn't sure. I anointed him with oil and made the sign of the cross on his head, declaring Christ's forgiveness through what He had done on the cross. I then asked Jesus to make Peter clean inside where he felt dirty. Peter said that he felt such stillness that he felt he almost didn't need to breathe. I suggested that although he didn't feel the need to, it was quite important that he did! We all laughed and thanked Jesus for His healing.

When Jesus is healing someone emotionally it is common to actually feel His compassion. It is very different from human empathy or feelings of emotion. It is wonderful! Remember that every person is a unique creation. This means that Jesus may heal people with the same emotional hurt or physical need in a completely different way. We must be careful not to make a formula or a set pattern that we keep to each time we pray for a person. The journey into healing needs to be led by the Lord, not by us following a prescription.

I am still hungry for more healing to take place, even though I have witnessed miraculous healings many times, and I pray God will use me more and more as I minister to people.

TaKING IT OUt tHeRe!

The late John Wimber often said, "The meat is on the street." It seems that unbelievers are, ironically, often the most open to healing. It often seems far easier to minister healing to people on the streets than to people in churches, as they have less hang-ups. In fact, if you want to start seeing people healed, first go and pray for people on the streets. You will be so encouraged. It gets such quick results! For the past couple of years a team from our church has been praying for people in the centre of our town.

This ministry, called "Healing on the Streets", has been operating very powerfully in Northern Ireland for the past few years. A team came to our church from there to encourage us to take part. Personally, I have only been out twice doing it, but it was very encouraging both times. The prayers are very short, ministering the power, love and healing of Jesus, and some people come back several weeks after they have been healed of some physical ailment, bringing other concerns relating to their family life for prayer. At first it was a little embarrassing to ask people if they wanted prayer for healing, but it is worth it when they are healed! Although we may be scared, the people who approach us just see the banner saying "Healing" in large letters and take it at face value. They believe us when we say Jesus can heal people today just as He did when He walked the earth. We need to not just believe it, but step out and start doing it. If you never do it, you'll never see it!

One of the things I said many years ago to Jesus was, "I am willing to be a fool for you." This means I have to forget myself and be willing to go with the flow of the Holy Spirit, ignoring the sense of embarrassment and what others might think. I remind myself that the person I am ministering to is the most important person in the world. His or her needs are more urgent than mine. It is not about my needs being met through the privilege of ministry, it's about the fact that Jesus died for that person and they need to know it. I just want to be a channel for Jesus to reveal His love to people.

OUR PERSONAL WALK WITH JESUS

When we use any of the gifts of the Holy Spirit we need to stay clean and keep short accounts with God. Confession, worship, reading the Bible and spending time with Him are all crucial to a fruitful life. Practise keeping in tune with the Holy Spirit out of love, not duty. The spiritual gifts function within a relationship, not like a slot machine we go and use when we feel like it. Practise being still and just "be" in God's presence, rather than coldly coming to Him with a list of your wants. Practise His presence and enjoy His closeness. Ask Him daily to show you how to love people.

Start reading the gospels again, focusing especially on the healing stories, letting them excite you afresh. Imagine yourself there watching Jesus minister, asking Him questions about what He is doing and why. Take time to read and study other books on the subject of healing, asking the Holy Spirit for fresh revelation. You may wonder why God does not heal everyone and it may help you to read the late John Wimber's testimony of how he prayed for at least 200 people before he saw his first healing.

Remember that when Jesus ministered, He sometimes had to pray for a person more than once. The blind man who saw people as "trees walking" needed more prayer from Jesus, as the healing was incomplete the first time. If Jesus had to pray more than once, we must not be surprised if we need to do the same, and more!

some Quick stories

I did not want to end the chapter without a few more opportunities to give God some glory! So here are a few quick testimonies of healings:

My husband once prayed for someone with tennis elbow. After a while he asked if the person was feeling anything, to which the person replied, "Yes, it feels a bit better." Ken prayed some more and all the pain and inflammation left completely.

A man Ken prayed for some time ago had a painful right ankle. After prayer he said that to his surprise, the left side of his body, that had always been painful and weak, had been healed instead! When my husband asked him why he hadn't mentioned that before, he replied that he had simply got used to living with it. As I said before, you never know what the Lord will do!

As I write, I am at Soul Survivor Festival in Somerset. Yesterday, we saw loads of people get healed in a seminar as young people laid hands on anyone who had physical complaints or emotional pain. They had all come up in answer to words of knowledge that had been given out by other young people. It was very exciting to see and hear what was going on. A lot of people had never prayed in this way before, such as speaking to medical conditions or painful limbs. Jesus loves involving willing people to work with Him.

THE KINGDOM OF GOD

When Jesus had called the Twelve together, he gave them power and authority to drive out all demons and to cure diseases, and he sent them out to proclaim the kingdom of God and to heal the sick.

Luke 9:1–2

Jesus never said that *all* the sick would be healed, but that every healing is a sign of the kingdom of God and that it is here amongst us, though it has not yet fully materialized. Jesus promised to return one day, and then all pain, sickness and crying would be things of the past. The old order would pass away (Revelation 21:4).

When Jesus finally comes in His fullness, all believers will be made whole. Our bodies will be raised into a resurrected body, into a glorious state, from weakness to power, from impure to pure, from mortal to immortal. Our bodies, which wear out and die, will then last forever (1 Corinthians 15:42–55). What a great and glorious day that will be, when we will join together with all the saints, serving and worshipping God Almighty!

PRAYER

Prayer for healing: Jesus, I look to You for my healing. You know what I need and You know why. Holy Spirit, please minister to me. I choose to trust You. I give You permission to come into my mind, memories and emotions. Surface those things that I have shut away. Bring to mind the things that You want to release and heal. Counsel and comfort me, dear Holy Spirit. Take me on a journey to wholeness. Amen.

Prayer to receive gifts of healing: Lord, thank You for all the times You have brought healing into my life. As You bring me wholeness and set me free, I ask that You would use me to bring healing and freedom to others. Please give me Your heart of mercy and compassion for those in need. Give me boldness to offer to pray for anyone who is sick or needs Your freedom. Impart to me in Your name gifts of healing. You said, "heal the sick". I have nothing of my own, but what You give to me I will give. Empower me by

Your Holy Spirit to bind up the broken-hearted, to proclaim freedom for the captives and release from darkness for prisoners. Use me to glorify Your name to believers and unbelievers. In Your precious name. Amen.

ACTION

Jesus came to show us what the kingdom of God is like. When He healed people, they experienced more than just one healing at a time – they would be made completely whole. Whatever we need to be healed from, we can guarantee that God wants us to experience complete freedom. That is what Jesus achieved for us on the cross and it is by His injuries inflicted there that we are made well.

What do you need healing for today? If it is a physical condition, place your hand on the appropriate area. Invite the Holy Spirit to come. Think of that part of your body in full working order. Thank Jesus for this part of your body. Speak healing to it in Jesus' name out loud. Every day thank Jesus for this part of your body. Bless it in Jesus' name. Receive His healing.

SCRIPTURES

He said, "If you listen carefully to the Lord your God and do what is right in his eyes, if you pay attention to his commands and keep all his decrees, I will not bring on you any of the diseases I brought on the Egyptians, for I am the Lord, who heals you."

Exodus 15:26

He heals the brokenhearted and binds up their wounds.

Psalm 147:3

... how God anointed Jesus of Nazareth with the Holy Spirit and power, and how he went around doing good and healing all who were under the power of the devil, because God was with him.

Acts 10:38

... to another faith by the same Spirit, to another gifts of healing by that one Spirit...

1 Corinthians 12:9

But he was pierced for our transgressions, he was crushed for our iniquities; the punishment that brought us peace was on him, and by his wounds we are healed.

Isaiah 53:5

...and begged him to let the sick just touch the edge of his cloak, and all who touched it were healed.

Matthew 14:36

He sent out his word and healed them; he rescued them from the grave.

Psalm 107:20

When Jesus had called the Twelve together, he gave them power and authority to drive out all demons and to cure diseases, and he sent them out to proclaim the kingdom of God and to heal the sick.

Luke 9:1–2

The Spirit of the Sovereign Lord is on me, because the Lord has anointed me to proclaim good news to the poor. He has sent me to bind up the brokenhearted, to proclaim freedom for the captives and release from darkness for the prisoners, to proclaim the year of the Lord's favor and the day of vengeance of our God, to comfort all who mourn, and provide for those who grieve in Zion – to bestow on them a crown of beauty instead of ashes, the oil of joy instead of mourning, and a garment of praise instead of a spirit of despair. They will be called oaks of righteousness, a planting of the Lord for the display of his splendor...

Instead of your shame you will receive a double portion, and instead of disgrace you will rejoice in your inheritance. And so you will inherit a double portion in your land, and everlasting joy will be yours.

Isaiah 61:1–3, 7

Now, Lord, consider their threats and enable your servants to speak your word with great boldness. Stretch out your hand to heal and perform signs and wonders through the name of your holy servant Jesus.

Acts 4:29–30

CHAPTER 12

INTRODUCING PRAYER MINISTRY

They will place their hands on sick people, and they will get well.

Mark 16:18

WHAT IS PRAYER MINISTRY?

Prayer ministry is not praying for someone *at a distance*. When we pray this way, we are praying *about* someone, not ministering the love of Jesus *to* them. Prayer ministry is prayer that is up close and personal. It is ministering in the power of the Holy Spirit and allowing ourselves to be used by God as a vessel or a channel of His love and power to work in someone's life. It is a power ministry of the Holy Spirit, not a time for wordy prayers. When we are involved in praying for people in ministry situations, we do not have to try and persuade Jesus to heal people – we are bringing His healing love and power *to* people. In the verse above, Jesus told His disciples to lay hands on the sick, and they would get well. It was God's power and might that would change people's lives, not the words of man. I am so thankful that this is the case!

There is something really heartening in seeing the body of Christ minister to each other and I am certain that it pleases God too. Of course, it is an essential part of body ministry within the church, but how much more must it please Him when He sees us doing it *outside* the church, just like Jesus and the disciples did!

In those days, there were no manuals on the "ABC of Prayer Ministry". Jesus and the disciples (after Pentecost) all relied on the empowering and prompting of the Holy Spirit, not a formula.

So do not worry if you feel "under-qualified" in all areas of prayer ministry. You do not need to be experienced to start laying hands on people, because it is the Holy Spirit who is ministering healing through you.

WHEN THE MIND IS TOO BUSY

When a leader or speaker invites people to come forward to receive prayer, it is helpful to understand what may be going through the minds of the people needing prayer. There are hundreds of different reasons why someone reaches out for ministry at any given time and it may be a battle for them to even rise up out of their chair. At other times, the Holy Spirit can propel them forward as the anointing falls on them to receive healing. Whatever the reason, be aware of the following battle that can rage in the minds of people as they come forward for prayer ministry:

- It's me again! I am always coming up for prayer. Everyone will think I have terrible problems.
- God may be too busy with the needs of others to give me any attention.
- What if nothing happens? I'm not expecting it to – nothing ever seems to work.
- I do not want to fall over!
- I feel vulnerable and hope I am not ambushed by one of those prophetic people who will tell me what I have to do.
- I know what I need and I do not want God to speak to me about anything else.

- I just want to be free. Will I ever be free?

In fact, you may have thought some or all of these things yourself, prior to receiving ministry.

So much can swirl around in our heads at times like this, that often we need to dial down a bit and relax to experience the presence of Jesus. This is actually crucial. More than anything, it is Jesus we want. It's not about a "power encounter" for its own sake; it's about meeting with Jesus.

BeInG StILL

Would you like to practise that right now? Maybe your mind is so full today that you are finding it difficult to concentrate as you read this book.

Why don't you invite His Holy Spirit to come to you and then just be still? Focus your thoughts on Jesus, without praying, simply being aware of Him. Sense Him standing near you. If you find this difficult then imagine Jesus on the cross, dying for you. Now repent of anything you may have said or done to grieve Him. Offer your whole being – emotions, intellect, hopes and dreams, disappointments and pains – to His care. You do not need to strive in this; instead do it from a place of stillness, calm and trust. Some people find it difficult to be still and do nothing. It can take time and practice, especially if life is busy and there is a lot of stress. It is tempting to think of all the prayers we *should* pray and all the things we *should* do, rather than taking time just being with Him.

So now, just enjoy His closeness for a while. The Bible tells us to "Be still and know that I am God" (Psalm 46:10), and it is enough to do just that.

You will find that your soul, mind, body and spirit all feel refreshed by being in His presence. It is wonderful!

This is how we want others to encounter the presence of

Jesus when we minister to them. It is important that we have experienced it ourselves on a regular basis so that we can recognize whether someone is encountering God or not. If they are not, you will need to lead them into stillness.

PRAYING FOR PEOPLE

The remainder of this chapter will focus on how to pray for people. We will look at some of the common questions asked and I hope to answer them in order to equip you to launch out into prayer ministry. I will also give some practical guidelines for prayer ministry, most of which have been outworked in my own life as I have been serving the Lord in this way.

This chapter should really have a warning attached to it: "Beware! Prayer Ministry Can Be Addictive!" It certainly is to me. It is such a wonderful ministry to be involved in. What could be better than seeing the church becoming whole, as it is designed to be? What could be more exciting than being out on the streets ministering the way Jesus and His disciples did, seeing signs and wonders take place? What could be more effective than unbelievers being healed and asking, "Who is this Jesus who heals people?"

THE CONFIDENCE ISSUE

When we are praying for people we might be distracted by so many undermining thoughts buzzing round in our heads, such as:

- What if nothing happens?
- What if something happens and I don't know what to do?
- What if the person thinks I am no good at praying?
- What if there is an evil spirit present?
- I am really not very good at this!
- I wish so-and-so was here instead of me!

- What if it's not God's will to heal this person?
- Jesus will not use me because I am not a very good Christian.

Let me answer these concerns in order to encourage you and impart hope to you.

WHat IF NOtHING HaPPens?

Something always happens! It might not be what the person has asked for or what you wanted to happen, but that is not your responsibility, it is the Lord's. He wants that person to be whole much more than you do, so all you have to do is be obedient to His word and lay hands on them.

WHat IF SOMEtHING HaPPens and I DON't KNOW WHat to DO?

This is not an exam! It is good to remember how weak you really are, because it is *God's* power that is made perfect in weakness. You can only do what the Father wants to do, so ask Him. Be willing to be a fool for Christ's sake. We do not have to have all the answers. Recognize that sometimes we may get it wrong, but there is grace to cover it all. God will show you what to do at the time. Try not to panic, but remember to be still in His presence.

WHat IF tHey tHINK I am NO GOOD at PRayING?

Lay your reputation on the line. Do not be afraid of man; just be obedient to the Lord. The person has come forward for healing, not to judge you and your prayers. It is an encounter with God that they need, so be faithful in leading them towards Him.

WHat IF tHeRe IS an evIL SPIRIt PResent?

Greater is He that is in you than he that is in the world. If there is no one more experienced you can call on, you can say the following: "I bind anything contrary to the Holy Spirit", and then pray the peace of Jesus on the person. Speak to your leader, who may take over or tell you of someone else with more experience who could meet with the person at another time.

I am not very good at this!

You might not be good at it, but the Holy Spirit is! When your mind speaks negatively, tell yourself to *stop it* and begin to ask the Holy Spirit what He wants you to do next. Remember, the truth is that with Him all things are possible and nothing is too difficult.

I wish so-and-so was here instead of me!

Jesus can use anyone for anything. The reality is, we often learn more by being flung in at the deep end than taking years to learn a formula. Think of Peter walking on the water. Jesus soon rescued him when he thought he was sinking. All the gifts of the Holy Spirit are available to all of us all the time. He will determine when we need them. So bring any spiritual inferiority to Jesus and surrender it to Him, because He does not want you to live under the enemy's lies.

What if it is not God's will to heal this person?

Healing has always been and always will be in the heart of God. The fact that we don't always see people healed shouldn't rob us of this truth. When we are doing His will and His work, we must be content to leave the outcome with Him.

Jesus is not going to use me because I am not a very good Christian

Compared to Jesus, no one is good enough! We are all like "clay pots" in His hands. He uses us as His vessels, but sometimes our feelings of inferiority can get in the way. Bring that to Jesus at the cross now, surrender it to Him. Being humble does not mean putting ourselves down, it means being ready to give all the glory to God. Often the Holy Spirit will use us powerfully when we are feeling the least spiritual. It is His work, remember!

HOW DO I PREPARE?

Before going up to pray for someone at the end of a church service, I usually go through the following little checklist in my head. After ministering to people for a while, you will find that you do this almost automatically in a matter of seconds. It is as if these points become a way of life in ministry:

1. *I ask for cleansing from sin.* I want to be a clean vessel for Jesus to use.
2. *I ask for a fresh anointing of power to heal the sick in Jesus' name.* Nothing can be done in my own strength; it is only by His power.
3. *I remember the name of Jesus is the most powerful name.* I do not need to fear any other name because it is at the name of Jesus that every knee will have to bow (Philippians 2:10–11). I have Someone working in me and with me who is greater than he who is in the world (1 John 4:4). So I do not fear the enemy or any demonic spirits when I am ministering to people in His name. The power of God is greater, so I can minister in confidence!
4. *I affirm that all healing is to be done in the name of Jesus.* I will not waste words, because Jesus never did. It is His name that breaks the power of sickness. Neither will I say to people that they have been healed – I will always ask them how they feel. If they are taking medication for a condition, encourage them to go back to their doctor.
5. *I agree that all power and authority belongs to Jesus.* When a policeman wears his uniform we know he has authority. People will respond to his authority because of it. A driver will stop driving his car at the policeman's request

when he sees the uniform, but the policeman cannot stop the car himself through brute force. The car would run him over! In the same way, we are clothed in Christ. He is our uniform and we have been given the authority in His name to heal the sick and set the captives free. But the power belongs to *Him*, working through us for His glory.

Receive His power and authority afresh right now by praying the following prayer:

Please come, Holy Spirit, and cleanse me. Thank You Jesus, for what You did for me on the cross. Thank You that all power and authority belongs to You. I declare that the Name of Jesus is the Name above all other names! All power and authority belong to Jesus. I ask you, Lord Jesus, to impart to me the power and authority in Your Name to heal the sick, cast out demons and set the captives free. I lay hold of it now for Your glory and honour. Thank You, Lord. Amen.

1. *I put on my spiritual ears and eyes.* I want to actively listen to the Holy Spirit and see what He is doing in a person. I will ask the Holy Spirit to show me what He sees and help me to hear what He is saying, shutting out any negative or distracting thoughts.
2. *I ask Jesus to help me every step of the way.* I want to rely on Jesus, leaning into Him, learning from Him. Sometimes He prayed for someone more than once to receive healing, so I will stay open and willing to spend more time with someone I am praying for. People may also receive their healing away from the meeting, which is why I am looking to Jesus to always lead me as I pray. I do not have a set pattern because everyone's needs are different and Jesus knows what those needs are.

WHEN IT IS TIME TO PRAY FOR PEOPLE

Here are some things to remember that will help when you are involved in prayer ministry:

1. Keep your eyes open so that you can see what the Holy Spirit is doing.
2. Stand to the side or in front of the person, not behind them.
3. Lay a hand gently on the person's head or shoulder.
4. Invite the Holy Spirit to come upon the whole person (mind, body, emotions, will).
5. Make sure that there is at least one ministering person of the same sex as the person you are ministering to. Be aware that the person you are ministering to may be vulnerable and could have been abused. Be sensitive to the fact that having someone of the opposite sex praying for them may be disturbing to them. Realize that a prayer ministry time involving people of the opposite sex can easily develop into something that ends up being sinful if safeguards are not taken. If you are in a conference or a public meeting, be aware that we always need to be *seen* to be doing what is right, not just doing what is right.

Here are some of the things I try to do when praying for someone who needs physical and/or emotional healing:

1. Ask the person's name.
2. Ask what they want Jesus to do for them.
3. Invite the Holy Spirit to come upon the whole person in the name of Jesus.
4. Wait for the Holy Spirit to begin working.
5. Keep your eyes open so that you can see what the Holy Spirit is doing, and also watch the person's body language – look out for contortions or expressions on their face etc.
6. Look for signs of the Holy Spirit on the person.
7. Ask the Holy Spirit to come into the mind, the emotions

and the will – every part of the person.

8. If they are also praying (look for their mouth moving) as you minister, then suggest to them that they receive rather than pray.
9. Ask for more power. Encourage the person to receive by saying something like, "Just receive" or "Let Jesus do what He wants".
10. Wait expectantly.
11. Ask the Lord to show you in some way what He is doing.
12. Ask the Holy Spirit, "What is the root cause?" (if appropriate).
13. I often ask Him, "Do you want to say something, Lord?"
14. If it's a physical condition, then speak to the condition in Jesus' name: "I speak healing to this knee in the name of Jesus" or "I speak to this broken bone in the name of Jesus and tell it to be healed."

Keep tracking what the Holy Spirit is doing. We only have authority to do what we see the Father doing. Ask throughout the prayer time, "What are you doing, Lord?" Watch for body language – the tightening of hands etc. Remain open to the leading of the Holy Spirit.

Here is a little format that may help you remember these things: W.E.L.L.:

Wait
Engage
Look
Listen

SOME SIGNS OF THE PRESENCE OF THE HOLY SPIRIT

- A sheen on person's face.
- A look of being engaged with God – a sense of peacefulness.
- Shaking.

- Trembling.
- Falling to the floor.
- Eyelids fluttering.
- Uncontrolled laughter.
- Tears.
- Breathing heavily.
- Rippling of the body.
- Crying loudly.
- Groaning.
- Jerking.

GIVING A WORD

If you get a word, a picture or a prophecy for the person you are ministering to, remember to offer it sensitively. It is not always appropriate to say it the minute you receive it. If the word, for instance, is revealing some insecurity, you can always try it out by praying it before actually saying it. For instance, "Jesus, please come and minister to all insecurity, especially anything in the area of..." – watching the reaction of the person to the prayer. You can then ask them if they struggle with insecurity and if they say that they do, you can offer the word at that point.

Remember, if you feel too nervous to take the plunge, you can always ask the person being ministered to a question. For instance, if you get a word of knowledge that someone had a difficult time during childbirth, you can start off by asking the question, "Have you any children?" and gradually lead in. It is better to go carefully as we learn, being encouraged bit by bit, rather than being stopped at the first post because we make a few mistakes and the person we are praying for has clearly "switched off".

SOME PHYSICAL RESPONSES TO PRAYER

Sometimes we can notice that someone is clenching and unclenching their hands. This may indicate frustration or anger. Ask the person if she/he is thinking/feeling anything in particular. If they say anger or frustration, ask them where they can feel it. It is usually in their stomach. Ask them to put their hand there and place your hand on top. Or place your hand in the small of their back – it seems to have the same effect. Ask Jesus to surface the anger and disperse it. Encourage the person to let it surface. There may be memories attached, so encourage the person to open these up to Jesus.

Sometimes you will see someone's eyeballs moving under their eyelids. This usually means that they are seeing something – re-living a memory or seeing a picture – so ask them what they are seeing. If appropriate, ask Jesus to come into their memories and to bring His healing. This can then lead on to deeper ministry, including the releasing of forgiveness.

TAKE CARE

One of the things we never tell people is that they have a demon or an evil spirit in them. This just creates fear in people and it may cause the person to avoid ministry in the future. There is also the danger that we could be wrong. People often make strange noises or cries of agony when they are releasing pain from past hurt, which is not, in itself, an evidence of demonic activity. It is true, of course, that sometimes people need deliverance from demons, but this is better referred to the leadership, who will have more experience in these matters.

FORGIVENESS

Time and time again I have seen how the whole area of unforgiveness can keep a person in bondage. Below I have included some prayers which are a helpful starting point in accessing the truths around forgiveness for a person who is locked up. We must never force people to forgive before they are really ready, otherwise it will mean they are just going through the motions without a deep heart change.

We must also be sensitive to where people are at before suggesting they forgive someone during prayer ministry. They may be angry with themselves and bitter about someone else's treatment of them. People can be easily damaged by someone insisting that they forgive another person if no recognition is given to the immense amount of suppressed pain that needs to surface in the process. I want to reiterate that, yes, forgiveness needs to take place, but the person's acknowledgment of pain or anger is of great importance. Again, sometimes the pain or anger is buried so deep that it may take time for it to surface over a longer period. It may not all happen during just one ministry time. Encourage the person that it is a good thing to release pain or suppressed anger from the past. Let them take it at their pace.

If the person is ready and willing to release their unforgiveness, you can suggest that you lead them in the following prayer as you pray for them. Encourage them to say the prayer out loud, as it is a declaration to the Lord (and to the enemy) that they want to be free:

> Dear Jesus, please forgive me for my deep-rooted anger, hatred and bitterness towards... [name the person]. I am so sorry. I repent of it and release the one who has hurt me into Your capable hands. I will not bind them to me any more. I choose to bring this all to the foot of Your cross. Please forgive me and release me now. Amen.

Encourage the person to receive the forgiveness of Jesus and, if appropriate, pronounce His forgiveness over them as follows:

> The blood of Jesus Christ, God's Son, cleanse you from all sin. I pronounce the forgiveness of Jesus over you now. Receive His forgiveness now with thankfulness in your heart.

You might also sign the person on the forehead with the sign of the cross, saying:

> I sign you with the sign of the cross – the sign of His peace and reconciliation.

At this point the person may have already released some pain and they may be weeping. Encourage them to continue to release forgiveness to those who have hurt them. It may help them to release to the one who has hurt them the forgiveness that they have just received. It usually helps for them to say out loud:

> In Jesus' name I choose to forgive you, [name the person] for [they need to speak out what the person did to them].

At this point more tears and pain may be expressed. If the person finds it difficult, assure them that forgiveness is a choice. Not only that, but it is a commandment of Jesus. By forgiving someone, it does not mean that what was done to us was right. It simply means that we choose to be free from the poison of unforgiveness in our lives.

You do not have to go it alone. It is usually a great idea to minister in twos, as that way you can encourage one another. It is good to celebrate with someone when God is on the move. It also offers protection and accountability, saving you from being unnecessarily exposed or vulnerable to attack. Remember to honour the person you are praying for by not gossiping with others about their lives.

As mentioned previously, the enemy will always try and get to you by one of two ways. He will either tell you that you are amazing at ministry or absolutely useless. Praying with someone else means that you can always pray for each other if one of you has been affected by the ministry. It also means that more gifts of the Holy Spirit will be in operation.

Always minister to others as you would like to be ministered to yourself, and remember to encourage each other as we say "Yes!" to being used by the Lord. Let's go for it!

Let the adventure begin!